CO-CONSTRUCTING THERAPEUTIC CONVERSATIONS
A Consultation of Restraint

Ivan B. Inger, Ph.D.
Co-Director, Family Studies Institute, Portland, Oregon,
and Clinical Psychologist and Family Therapist in Independent Practice

Jeri Inger, M.S.
Co-Director, Family Studies Institute, Portland, Oregon,
and Marriage and Family Therapist in Independent Practice

Foreword by
David Campbell & Ros Draper

Systemic Thinking and Practice Series
Series Editors
David Campbell & Ros Draper

Karnac Books
London 1992 New York

First Published in 1990 by DC Publications

Published in 1992 by
H. Karnac (Books) Ltd.
58 Gloucester Road,
London SW7 4QY

Distributed in the United States of America by
Brunner/Mazel, Inc.
19 Union Square West
New York, NY 10003

ISBN 1 85575 023 6

A CIP catalogue record for this book is available from the British Library.

Printed in Great Britain by BPCC Wheatons Ltd, Exeter

CONTENTS

EDITORS' FOREWORD

We have known Jeri and Ivan Inger for several years through our jointly organised family therapy exchange in Britain, the United States and Denmark. As co-founders of The Family Studies Institute in Portland, Oregon, they are experienced as teachers, supervisors and practitioners of systemic family therapy.

We are very pleased to publish this book, making an exciting contribution to the development of the current wave of systemic thinking. When we first saw them work we were struck by the way they enacted systemic thinking in their family therapy sessions. It seemed to us that theoretical underpinnings of the systemic approach such as dissolving the problem system, making new connections and leading family members to an observer position, were happening before our eyes. Theory and practice had become one.

The format of this book captures the essence of their work. Since, similar to a family's experiences, much of it cannot be described, the

Ingers offer a detailed commentary on a transcript of a consultation session with a family. They demonstrate through a group discussion the way they generate systemic understanding, and the book closes with a presentation of the theoretical background to their work. In spite of their background as Milan systemic therapists, their approach creates a bridge between systemic thinking and other approaches such as communication theory, Gestalt, the use of metaphor, play and humour, and it is truly integrative.

We feel this book is very important as an intervention to the family therapy field. The Ingers demonstrate here that as systemic thinking and practice continue to evolve, workers can develop new techniques and integrate different approaches without giving up their basic foundation of systemic thinking.

David Campbell,
Ros Draper

ACKNOWLEDGEMENTS

We thank David Campbell and Ros Draper for suggesting and encouraging us to undertake this project. Their faith in our work has meant a great deal to us. We also thank all the participants in the Exchange Program: Chris Farmer, June Henley, Marlene Jones, Barry Mason, Colette Richardson, Paddy Sweeney and Doug van Loo from Britain and Ireland and Sandra Baker, Robert Beatty, Marcia Benedict, Marti Bradley-Kufchak, Teri Campbell, Mary Denevan, Carolyn Goolsby, George Hannibal, Karen Markham, Kathleen McGlaughlin, Eddi Miglavs, Doug Pullin and Alan Weisbard from the United States. Our special thanks to Silvia Nobori for bringing the family for an interview. We thank Ray and Nancie Gertler and the Bend, Oregon Family Therapy Group, and, finally, we offer special thanks to Virginia Shabatay, a learned scholar on the subject of Martin Buber.

I. B. I.
J. I.

Introduction:
theoretical considerations

We believe that as therapists it is important that the methods we use reflect our own belief systems and that our ideas and our interactions with families about those ideas be coherent. We claim an approach called an aesthetic preference (Allman, 1982; Keeney, 1983) as opposed to that of an applied science approach or belief system. Family therapists who subscribe to an applied science belief system identify with values associated with the physical sciences and are concerned with the control of nature for practical purposes. Differences between applied science therapists and aesthetically oriented therapists often revolve around issues of power and control (Hoffman, 1985), differences about who or what "determines" change, and which methods are useful in facilitating change.

When we speak of an aesthetic preference, we are speaking of the ideas of Gregory Bateson about cybernetics or feedback functions of biological and social systems based on cognitive or mental organization (Bateson, 1972, 1979). We also call into service

1

the ideas of the new biologists or constructivists, Von Foerster (1981), Maturana (1978), Varela (1979), Maturana and Varela (1980) and von Glasersfeld (1984). Von Foerster proposed second-order cybernetics as opposed to first-order cybernetics of the "hard" sciences (Keeney, 1983; Hoffman, 1990). Second-order cybernetics requires that the observer or observing system be considered part of the whole. As Hoffman puts it:

> A second-order view would mean that therapists include themselves as part of what must change; they do not stand outside. [1990, p. 5]

As second-order family therapists, we work as guests of families in a foreign domain. As guests, we behave in a respectful manner towards our hosts. This attitude of respect requires that we learn their language and meanings. It is, therefore, our job to discover those meanings and to try to understand how they operate within the family. Meanings given to experiences depend upon the contexts within which they are experienced. Thus, our work with the family centres around understanding and inclusion (Buber, 1965, p. 97) of both their dynamics and their contexts. Inclusion and understanding are processes in which one acknowledges the legitimacy of the position of "the other" but does not necessarily endorse their position. This topic will be further discussed in the "Further Theoretical Considerations" section.

We find that in being part of the system, we are able to interact with families and co-construct meanings that come from that interaction. This languaging exchange or transformation of meanings must be conducted in a safe-enough environment. The process of making it safe-enough requires the therapist to take major responsibility for assuming an observing position separate from their own beliefs and those of the family. We introduce this reflective position into the dialogue by conversing with each other about our observations of the families' ideas and their meanings as they are put forth in the interview, interjecting, from time to time, our own meanings and, thus, planting the seeds of co-creation (Inger and Inger, 1990b).

In our work and our teaching, we use a two-person team in the room interviewing the family (Inger and Inger, 1990b). We see this as a way of translating Bateson's (1979) notions of double description into action. Bateson discusses this concept of double description by saying:

> It is correct (and a great improvement) to begin to think of two parties to the interaction as two eyes, each giving a monocular view of what goes on and, together, giving a binocular view in depth. This double view is the relationship. [Bateson, 1979, p. 133]

Two persons conjointly conducting the interview create information in-depth through complementary and symmetrical descriptions. Two therapists can have two different opinions or two matching opinions. Both interactions enhance the distinctions, descriptions and meanings around the family issues. By offering either symmetrical or complementary descriptions of the issues in continuous dyadic reflections throughout the interview, the two of us can create the necessary conditions for coupling between ourselves and the family. Our intentions are to help families transform their interactions from redundant patterns into interactions with new and different constructions of meanings which prove to be more useful to their relationships with each other than their, heretofore, redundant meanings with which they believed they were stuck.

The interview presented in the text represents many of the beliefs and methods presented above, and in the "Further Theoretical Considerations" section of the book. We will amplify ideas about the content/process recursion in therapy, the implications and consequences of the intentions of therapists on their interventive interactions with families, and we will discuss differential aspects of interpretation as they relate to a second-order cybernetic family therapy. Regarding the differential aspects of interpretation, we will discuss the importance of understanding and inclusion as being consistent with a second-order cybernetic therapy belief system.

The Consultation

This consultation is conducted with a family and their therapist as part of an Exchange Training Seminar (Inger, Inger and Baker, 1990a). This Exchange was an idea developed by co-trainers David Campbell and Ros Draper of London, England and ourselves, Ivan B. Inger and

Jeri Inger of Portland, Oregon. The participants were family therapists who were studying with us in Portland and London.

The Exchange was developed as a way to give therapists the
opportunity to practice their work in foreign countries and experience being guests in foreign cultures. It was a chance for us to be
immersed in a new culture, a new system, and a new way of working. As a result of being immersed, we experienced enhanced skills
of observering, and reflectivity. While all of these ideas pertained to
this Exchange, they also pertain to the work we do in family therapy
and to the foregoing presentation.

In July 1988, twelve Americans travelled to London where they
stayed with host colleagues and their families, went to work with
their fellow family therapists, and met with their British and Irish
counterparts in a five-day seminar to exchange ideas in new cross-
cultural ways.

In July 1989, Part II of the Exchange Training Seminar took place
in Portland, Oregon, in similar fashion to Part I. The same British
and Irish family therapists stayed with their American colleagues,
went to work with fellow family therapists, and came back together
to exchange ideas in the seminar. This consultation interview was
part of the five-day seminar.

The family of this interview is an American middle-class family.
It is the first marriage for both parents, and they have two children,
Barbara, the oldest, is 13 years old and Steven is seven years old.
Mother and Father are in their mid-thirties. They are fairly new to
Portland and the Northwest. They have each left their extended
families 3,000 miles away. As you will see from the dialogue, it is
still difficult to be pioneers in America. To this day each family
member is strongly influenced by their families and the cultural
pull of the East Coast. Father's family lives an upper-middle-class
lifestyle in the suburbs of New York City. They have no notion why
anyone would want to live anywhere else or in any other lifestyle.
Mother's mother has retired in warm and sunny Florida.

The family sought therapy at a youth services centre in the suburbs of Portland, where family therapist, Silvia Nobori, agreed to
see them. Their presenting problem was their daughter, Barbara.
She was lying and stealing, and Mother was concerned that she
would soon be out of the family's control. The latest catastrophe
was that Barbara was caught stealing from a store during her

wealthy paternal grandparents' visit, and just after her religious confirmation. In other words, a very important moment in the history of this family.

Part of our training program at The Family Studies Institute* includes simulating a family before meeting with them. Using the presenting data from the intake, we ask participants from the group to play the role of family members. They, along with the interviewers and observers, make up what we call "the team."

Simulating a family prior to interviewing them takes the team out of the intellectual arena of hypothesizing and into the experiential arena of action. It is the difference between "I wonder what would happen if . . ." and "look what happened when. . . ." The *as if* quality of hypothesizing is replaced with a simulated construction of the family. A reflective pre-picture is taken and developed. These developed pre-pictures indicate the repertoire of hypothesized pictures prior to the family's corrections. Through dialogue, these preconceived pictures are reconstructed as a picture that makes sense to both of them.

Following the simulation and the interview, we explore this larger process in the Debriefing. By looking at our pre-pictures with their reconstructed pictures superimposed upon them, we are able to reflect and examine our work and our beliefs and the continuity between them.

In the simulation of this family, we asked several participants in the seminar to both play family members and to be "the team" for the interview. The simulated Mother felt a great deal of pressure to tell the therapists about Barbara's stealing. Her first lines were:

I am concerned about Barbara, and I need some help. Our dilemma is that we have a daughter who is doing things like

---

*The Family Studies Institute is a small training organization located in Portland, Oregon. It is committed to the cybernetic view of the family as a self-organizing, interdependent system whose members are linked in an ongoing developmental process. Inherent in the training is the notion that families are subcultures within subcultures, within the larger culture, and, thus, cross-cultural learning is imperative. Also, the institute is committed to community service. This includes both working with families in the community using a sliding fee schedule and offering community educational programs.

stealing. She was a great little girl, and she has changed. She's getting out of control. I'm scared. I'm the mother and she does not listen to me.

By divulging this private information about her daughter and by declaring Barbara *the* dilemma or problem, Mother set the scene for the entire interview. We found that the embarrassment was overwhelming for the simulated Barbara, and it was impossible to make contact with her after that. Our inability to make contact with Barbara encouraged her simulated Mother to organize the interview around Barbara's negative attributes.

This exercise allowed us to hypothesize about the possible danger of allowing either the therapist or the parents to divulge this embarrassing incident too soon. We began to see the need to restrain ourselves, Silvia, the therapist, and the parents from this divulgence, as a way of trying to preserve the therapeutic alliance for family and therapist. It has been our experience that when parents come to an interview and immediately dominate the conversation, a symmetrical conversation among the adults occurs and leaves the children as outsiders to that conversation. Our intention is to include children from the beginning, and to create a safe-enough environment for them to participate. Parents who insist on invoking their prerogatives in the conversation, and who present their child(ren) using negative attributions, can be a challenge and must be handled diplomatically and positively. We do not want to inadvertently insult the parents in their role as parents.

We hypothesized that the actual interview would require a great deal of restraint, that is, restraining our own need to know, as well as restraining the Mother's need to tell. If we were successful, we might create a productive process in which new and different options for interaction could be introduced into the family repertoire. If we were unsuccessful in averting the Mother's litany of Barbara's negative attributes, we might get stuck in content. We consider content to be the subject matter of the dialogue, and process to include all those words we might use to describe the way we carry on the dialogue. We thought that by controlling the pace we might be able to help Barbara escape the role of symptom bearer. As you will see in the interview, we do that by interrupting, talking to each other, repeating family member's words and phrases, and getting confused. Slowing down the pace of the dialogue allows the family to hear themselves and to hear us, and, thus, be more thoughtful and open to new responses. One way or another, our intentions were to take charge of the flow of information and create a safe-enough environment for each member of the family.

The Format of the Presentation

The verbatim presentation of the interview is on the left-hand side of each page, and an annotation of the interview is on the right-hand side. The annotation contains our thoughts about our experience of this interview and the meanings we attribute to the interactions as they evolve. We present the process of developing the intervention with a team of participants, the presentation of the intervention, and the debriefing session that followed.

The reader will find that just as the dialogue flows freely between us when we talk with a family, so does the annotation. It will shift back and forth between the two of us, reflecting our points of view, without constantly announcing the shift.

The second section of the book contains the theoretical perspective upon which we base our work. We began exploring a systemic or cybernetic approach to family therapy fifteen years ago, and we have developed many theoretical ideas and applications since then (Inger and Inger, 1990a, 1990b). Some of our methods centre around the two-person team and the coherence that it provides for the family, second-order cybernetic beliefs (especially as they relate to Martin Buber's notion of inclusion [Buber p. 97]), and the use of metaphor as part of the coupling process in the dialogic interplay. We subscribe to the idea of self-healing tautologies and, thus, reject the use of power and control in favour of restraint.

Working with the circular relationship between content and process and the incorporation of the observing/reflecting position have been two of the most fascinating aspects of our work with families. All of these concepts will become clearer as you wend your way through the interactions of content and process in the interview with us.

Transcript of a consultation with a therapist and a family

During the morning session of the Exchange Seminar, Silvia Nobori, the family's therapist, presented her impressions of the family and her work with them to the Exchange participants. Shortly after her presentation, participants simulated the family, and we conducted the interview with them. The actual family was interviewed the same afternoon. Below is the information that Silvia shared with the simulators.

The Therapist's Presentation of the Family

Jeri: Silvia, tell us about the family.

Silvia: This is a family of four; Mother and Father are in their mid-thirties, Barbara is 13 years old, and Steven is seven years old. Mother called requesting family therapy. Mother is mostly concerned about Barbara's stealing. Barbara was picked up for shoplifting two days after her religious confirmation while her paternal grandparents were visiting from New York. That was

8

the precipitating problem that pushed Mother into calling for family therapy. Barbara believes she and her brother should get the same number of gifts for their birthdays. However, she feels she should be special and get more time alone with her paternal grandparents. This poses a dilemma for the family because Mother says she shouldn't get more. At the same time, Barbara is stealing her possessions and invading other people's territories.

Mother works and Father is unemployed and a student. Father usually tries to remove himself from the family's dilemmas. He is gone a lot. When he is home, he is often outside playing ball with Steven. He does not seem surprised that his daughter misses him. He admitted he used to play with her a lot. Barbara's perception of the problem was that she lost her Father to Steven. Father validated this and said he doesn't know what to do with her now. They don't have anything in common.

I have seen the family three times, so I am just beginning to know them. Mother seems to feel she has lost her daughter to her husband's parents who are quite wealthy. In the last session, Barbara blurted out that she was having problems so her Mother and Father would not get divorced. She wrote her grandmother and asked if she could live with her if her parents divorced. Grandmother wrote back and said yes. Mother was quite upset and said she felt she lost Barbara as a result of this. She is afraid her mother-in-law may be able to "buy" the children. Mother recently had a hysterectomy and had to stay in bed a while. Barbara may have crossed Mother's boundary, by seeing herself as the Mother of the house.

Mother believes in therapy, so it wasn't unusual for her to agree to come today. Father is coming mostly to please his wife. Barbara doesn't want to come today, and Steven will be more of an observer. I've watched him play quietly and observe whatever they are doing and saying. Every once in a while he will comment. I framed their coming today as being helpful to our Exchange participants. I did not promise the family that they would get anything out of it, although I did say they might find it interesting. I told them that we would want feedback from them about what the experience was for them.

Ivan: Is there anything more you want to share with us?

Silvia: Mother has known her husband since she was 15 years old. She comes from a single-parent, working-class family and Father comes from a two-parent, wealthy family. He has two brothers and is the middle child. Mother's father died when she was seven years old, and she was raised alone by her mother. She is the youngest of four children and has three older brothers. She met her husband through her older brother who went to college with him and brought him home for a visit.

Interviewing the Family

The family, Mother, Father, Barbara and Steven, along with the therapist, Silvia, enter the room and sit on chairs facing the consultants, with their backs to the audience. We sit next to each other facing the family. Previous to entering the room, we had gone out to meet the family and briefly talked about the upcoming interview. The family have their backs to the audience. Steven does not sit in a chair, but immediately sits on the floor under a table out right. He proceeds to play with two little dolls that one of the participants had brought with her. Mother and Father sit next to each other, Mother on the left of Father, and Barbara on Father's right. To the left of Barbara is the therapist, Silvia.

Father is dressed neatly in a dark gray suit, and Mother is wearing a light gray dress. Barbara is dressed in a white cotton cardigan sweater, white T-shirt, white Bermuda shorts, and black shoes. Steven has on a T-shirt, shorts, and canvas shoes. The family at first appears quiet, cautious and, yet, nonverbally, give the impression they are ready to cooperate in the interview. Barbara smiles shyly at us, plays with her long, black hair, alternately tying it in a pony-tail, undoing it and then letting it fall down. Occasionally she shakes her head so her hair flies out. As it falls down over her shoulders, she bows her head, giving us the impression that she is both anxious and sad.

The family is seated with their backs to the audience, and we are facing the family and the audience. Mother is on the far left, followed by Father, then Barbara, and Silvia is on the far right. Steven is under the table to Ivan's right.

The Interview

Ivan: Silvia, could you share with us what your thoughts were about the family coming and how you thought this might be a useful experience.

Silvia: I thought it might be useful to us in the Exchange Training Program this week because it's important to talk with real families. I thought about this family because they are a very articulate family. They came in with some individual concerns and with some family concerns. I explained that this will not be therapy, but I hoped it would be interesting and helpful to them. They talked it over and decided to come today, although some members of the family want to be here more than others.

(pause)

Ivan: (Looking at Mother) You seem to know what she means by that. So he's the one? (Mother is looking at Steven who is under a table to the right of Ivan).

Mother: uh huh.

Ivan: Do the three of you all want to be here equally?

Our Annotations

Silvia, the family's therapist, is asked to present the family to us. She tells us about the purpose of the interview, while maintaining her alliance with the family.

The comment by the therapist that some members want to be here more than others is cryptic. Such a comment, which is rich in innuendo and pointedness cannot be ignored. It is the first emotionally charged issue presented to us. The fact that the therapist does not specifically state who does and does not want to be here leaves it up to us to explore. Hence, Ivan begins by asking about Steven and then about differences among the other three regarding who does and does not We often find it interesting to see whether there is continuity in the protestations. In this case, Barbara makes a shift in her position by the end of the interview

Barbara: (nods head no) ... uh uhh.

Ivan: You would not like to be here (looking at Barbara)?

Barbara: (nods yes — I would not like to be here)

Ivan: Where would you like to be?

Barbara: (Shrugs her shoulders but gives no verbal response)

We don't focus on the content of Barbara's refusal to talk, but we watch the process of Barbara's not talking and how it evolves in the developing context of the interview.

Jeri: Would you like to be here less than your brother, or more?

Barbara: Less.

This is an example of how a team of two can alternate asking about the same topic in a complementary way. In this way one interviewer need not take responsibility for one line of inquiry. Ivan is asking questions about options, while Jeri asks a question about comparison. Both of these kinds of questions could be categorized as Tomm's orienting questions (1987b, 1988).

Ivan: So how come he gets to be under the table?

Barbara: Cause he's littler.

Picking up on Silvia's presentation of Barbara's jealousy of Steven, Ivan comments about Steven being allowed to be under the table.

Ivan: (To Steven) So, when you get bigger you will have to stay in chairs?

(Steven does not respond or acknowledge the question but Barbara nods yes)

(pause)

We are trying to create permission for Steven to be where he is and trying to let him know that we will find a way to include him.

Not interfering with his behaviour is our way of communicating respect for and developing trust with family members. By talking about Steven being under the table, we are attempting to reassure Steven that we will not try to get him into a chair.

If your parents weren't in this kind of fishbowl (referring to the audience) would they be doing something different about Steven under the table or is this the way they would usually handle Steven?

Barbara: They would make him sit in the chair.

Ivan: They would make him sit in the chair.

Jeri: Mother asked me if it was OK and I kind of nodded. Maybe that's the difference today. She got some permission from me to let him be there.

Mother: If you don't need him to be sitting right here (in a chair), he'll play quietly by himself and not be

We often start an interview by relating to the children. We acknowledge the children, knowing that most often one of the children is the one considered by the parents and/or others to be the identified patient. This is our way of telling the children that we will relate to them with equity and respect. We will not side with parents just because we and they are adults.

disruptive. But if you need him to sit here, I can have him sit here.

Ivan: Do you think there would be anything that would be of interest to him to bring him over here?

Mother: No

Ivan: Nothing? Nothing you could think of that would be of interest?

Mother: No

Jeri: But, if we come to something of interest to us is it OK to ask him a question even though he's under the table?

Mother: Yes.

Father: Yes.

Mother: Steven, why don't you come up here and play with your toys instead of hiding over there.

(He complies and sits on the floor next to Mother's chair)

Jeri: Hmmm. That looked easy.

Ivan: (Talking to Jeri) So they (the children) came for a reason other than being interested.

Mother: Yeah. To check out the new toys.

Jeri: (To Steven) Is it OK if we ask you a question once in a while even though you are

Jeri seeks the parents permission to communicate with Steven. It implies respect for the parents as well as acknowledgement that they have control over Steven's place in the family and his place in the interview.

Jeri establishes what seems to be an acceptable means of communication with Steven.

down there? You will nod? Let me see. What is yes?

Steven: (He nods up and down).

Jeri: That's yes. OK. What is no?

Steven: (He nods sideways)

Jeri: Oh, good. OK . We've got it down now. As long as it's a yes and no question, we're all right.

We believe it is exceedingly important, in the beginning of an interview, to establish rapport and a level of communication that is acceptable to children. Otherwise, it often becomes an adult conversation with the children trailing behind, bored or trying to get into the conversation in ways that appear to be disruptive. By engaging in dialogue with children at the beginning, we lessen the acting-out on their part. In other words, children are given a legitimate status in the interview.

Ivan: Barbara, now that he's back here do you want to be here more or less than you did before?

Barbara: About the same.

Ivan: About the same? Nothing's changed? Your Mother made him an offer. She said why don't you come over here, and he came. She hasn't made you an offer yet. Is there an offer she could make that could make you want to be here more or less?

Barbara: No, I guess not.

Jeri: Nothing she could offer?

Mother: I guess if I offered her the choice to leave, she might leave.

Ivan comes back to the question of who wants to be here and who does not in order to find out what the nature of the process is going to be. By not attending to the question, it will linger and remain unknown. To let it linger and remain unknown means it will come back to "haunt" us in some way.

Ivan: She would? Where would she go?

Mother: She would wait out in the car.

Ivan: (to Barbara) Is that where you would go?

(To Mother) How about yourself?

Mother: I don't mind being here at all.

Ivan: You don't. Father, how about you?

Father: I don't mind being here at all.

Ivan: How come the two of you don't mind being here and the two children don't want to be here?

Father: I know he doesn't want to be here because he's pretty shy. He doesn't like a group of people.

Ivan: It could be pretty intimidating.

Mother: Barbara, probably because she thinks we are going to talk about her.

(Barbara whispers something that no one could hear.)

Ivan: What is it that we were going to talk about that is about you (to Barbara)? Would that be different, Barbara, than talking with you?

Up until now we have been engaging the children as a way of keeping the parents from embarrassing Barbara by confronting the issue of her being caught stealing. As long as Barbara was talking, they were listening. Now, Ivan begins to flirt with the danger of talking about secrets that Barbara does not want talked about. We must take certain chances in order to establish the patterns of dialogue that may or may not ensue. To avoid issues in silence is potentially destructive. Taking a chance can be a way of establishing parameters for the conversation. While restraining ourselves from pursuing the "it," we are probing, and externalizing the problem.

Barbara: (Shrugs her shoulders)

Father: (To Barbara) You can speak up.

Silvia: (To Ivan) I don't know if she knows what you meant by that.

Ivan: Did you?

Barbara: Uh huh.

Jeri: (To Barbara) Do you have any sense of what this is all about?

Barbara: (Shakes her head no)

Father: How about why you started going to see Silvia? Do you want to talk about it?

Barbara: (Shakes her head no vigorously, with hair flying)

This comment by Silvia lets Barbara know that she is looking out for her. In an attempt to help clarify the question, Jeri inadvertently pushes too hard. This encourages the Father to go after "it" again. This feels like a mistake to both of us. Ivan attempts to rectify it by interrupting the Father's confrontation with Barbara. Restraining the parents like this requires a delicate balance, and, when accomplished, allows children to experience the process very differently. In our attempt to block the parents from creating an Identified Patient, we must also restrain ourselves from our own curiosity. This process allows us to develop a trusting relationship with the children, thereby creating safety for everyone. This follows Tomm's idea (1987a, p. 4) that by restraining the family from talking about the symptoms, we can keep the symptoms from becoming respectable, and the dominant aspects of the conversation.

Ivan: Excuse me. I have to interrupt a moment. Do you mind if I talk to Jeri?

(Talking to Jeri) I'm wondering, if instead of our asking her all these questions, if she might help us by asking us a question.

Jeri: OK. Let's try it.

Ivan: Would you be willing to ask us a question?

Barbara: (Shrugs)

Ivan: Anything. Like, why did you wear your shirt today or something to help me because I'm nervous about all of this. I really could use a question to get me off the hook of your not being willing to answer questions.

Barbara: (Shrugs and sits passively)

(Silence)

Ivan: Do you have an answer for us maybe?

Barbara: (shakes her head no)

We are reflecting and the family is listening. This reflectivity is built into the fabric of the interview and becomes a part of its context. Reflectivity here is not formalized in the way that Andersen (1987) conducts the reflecting portion of the interview. We have discovered that this method of reflecting allows us to explore hypotheses, and invites the family to become a part of this process and to contribute to its refinement. Reflecting in this manner, we co-create the experience in alliance with the family.

Offering Barbara the option of asking the therapist questions is a way of empowering her, which she needed after the confrontation from her Father.

Ivan: You are clear about that. You have no answer. But you are not sure you have or do not have a question for us.

Barbara: No. I don't have a question!

Ivan: You don't have a question.

Jeri: How about for Silvia?

Barbara: (Shakes her head no)

Ivan: Not even a question of why did you do this to us (i.e., to bring us here)? Not even what was the matter with you. Were you thinking crazy one day . . .

(Barbara vigorously shakes her head no several times, but with a smile)

Jeri: How about your Mother and Father? No questions like what are you doing to me?

Ivan: (to Jeri) Is she always this good?

Jeri: I don't know.

Mother: I wish she was always this quiet.

Ivan: She's not always this quiet?

Mother and Father: No

Barbara's first sentence with an assertive voice! Successful verbal contact has been set up, and we are attempting to develop trust with her. This is the beginning of the first shift in the interview. Taking risks, while attempting to join Barbara, the Identified Patient, requires an attitude of experimentation.

Barbara makes a lot of playful contact with us, with her eyes and her body movements. She does not alienate us from her, in spite of her seeming refusal to be verbal. She seems to be playing with us.

Ivan uses the word "good" — not a common response for him. Perhaps he is still trying to pull Barbara out of the Identified Patient position that Mother and Father are trying so hard to keep her in.

Ivan is wondering out loud about Barbara. He uses Jeri instead of asking the parents directly, as a way of blocking their negative response about Barbara's behaviours.

Jeri: What do you think is making her more quiet here?

Mother: She's embarrassed.

Jeri: Oh! What do you think, Father?

Father: I think she's embarrassed 'cause she's never this quiet.

Asking parents why she is more quiet here is a way of positively connotating her quietude as well as helping them look at the context which quiets her down (positive attention).

The theme of the interview usually develops in the beginning. Embarrassment is one of the themes of this interview. We are beginning to see how much Barbara and her parents do to embarrass each other.

Jeri: She doesn't realize that they are all watching us and not her.

Ivan: Yes. You see we have to look good. We have an audience here. So you may not understand how nervous we are. We have to keep looking at them (the audience). I have to keep seeing if they are smiling or not.

If they frown I know I am not doing good. If they smile I think I might be doing good.

(To Barbara) Would you think it might help if you looked at them (the audience)? Just to sneak a look?

Barbara: (shakes her head no and refuses, and then sneaks a look)

We often tell clients that the audience is watching us, trying to learn from us as our way of taking some of the pressure off them. In this bit of dialogue, Ivan is making it clear that there are pressures on him to look good just as there are pressures on Barbara to interact. Ivan is joining Barbara in a symmetrical way.

We use our "selves" as an element in our interview. What we mean is that we put ourselves into the interview as a way of entering the subjective experience as participants. We make ourselves vulnerable to the forces of interaction and allow ourselves to step out of the role of disinterested expert. This allows for the co-creation of dialogue. Ivan is attempting to reframe the situation

Silvia: I thought maybe she might be curious. I know that before coming Barbara was curious.

Father: I can't believe you are not speaking! This is amazing!

Mother: Never when you want them to talk!

(Parents laugh)

Ivan: Or maybe she's offering you an opportunity to speak.

Mother: Want me to talk (asking Ivan)?

Ivan: Yes, if you wish.

Father: (To Barbara) You don't want to talk about why you went to see Silvia?

Mother: Should we start off with it?

Barbara: (Shakes her head no)

Mother: (To Barbara) Well, it's going to have to come out.

Barbara: (Continues to shake her head frantically)

Mother: Stop doing that!

Barbara: No!

Jeri: That makes me very curious. I'm wondering, if Barbara could talk to us, what she would say about the meaning of her silence.

Ivan: And the "what" is going to come out.

positively by suggesting that Barbara's silence is not necessarily negative. It does have positive implications as well. It can provide time for the parents to speak.

This is a difficult moment for us and, also, a typical dilemma for therapists: how to empower Barbara and, at the same time, not antagonize the parents. In response to our efforts, the parents are trying to keep Barbara in the Identified Patient position. Barbara is squirming, using head shaking to distract them. We are talking faster in an attempt to help Barbara remain empowered, without enraging her parents. They are determined to reveal her secret, and we are as determined to protect her. This is an example of a dilemma many therapists find themselves in vis à vis parents who seek coalition with therapists against a child.

Jeri: And why all the anxiety about it.

Ivan: Well, I'm anxious that it might be worse than I know. I don't know if I could handle it?

Barbara: (Shrugs her shoulders)

Amplifying the importance of the secret seems to create more distance from it, and by taking on and verbalizing the anxiety, we hope to relieve them of it. Talking about whether we could "handle it" brings us back from content to process, this unending recursion.

Ivan: (To Barbara) You don't know if I could handle It? Do you think you could handle it?

Barbara: (Shakes her head no)

Jeri: Is Silvia handling it?

Barbara: (Shakes her head yes, genuinely and enthusiastically)

Jeri: Oh, Good!

Ivan: Silvia is handling it.

Jeri: Yes.

Ivan: (To Jeri) So there is a privacy issue here. We ought to respect that.

Jeri: Indeed.

(Silence)

Empowering Barbara to tell Ivan whether he could not handle it is a way of getting Barbara to help us fend off the family secret. It is like helping her close the hamper on the family's dirty laundry.

Bringing Silvia into the dialogue is a way of reminding the family that there is a place for the dirty laundry other than in public. There are alternatives to this kind of embarrassment. Jeri's intervention punctuates Barbara's relationship with Silvia and reminds us that this interview is a consultation. Silvia is the primary therapist, and the one whose relationship with the family we must preserve. We want to avoid even the appearance of competing with the therapist for the allegiance of the family.

Ivan: (To Jeri) I think that is very important. It seems to

The parents freeze, and Barbara begins preening herself, pulling me that what Barbara is saying to us is that there is a privacy issue and that it is important for her to keep it private.

Mother: I think it is because she is embarrassed about the reason she had to come to see Silvia.

Jeri: (To Ivan) I wanted to ask Barbara some more questions about how Silvia is handling it, not what she is handling.

on her shorts and stroking her hair, almost as though there is a mirror in front of her.

The tension is growing. The Mother is pressing to expose the stealing, and we are trying to preserve the secrecy and thereby preserve Silvia's credibility with Barbara. Mother still does not want to give up on the content. She escalates again as she brings up Barbara's embarrassment about the reason she has to see Silvia.

We find that talking to each other slows the family down because they listen to us.

Jeri reconfirms the idea that Silvia is handling "it" with Barbara. This time she presents the idea to Ivan, hoping this dialogic process will help the family hear it. Thus, the client system moves into an observing system. They reflect on what they hear. It is not necessary that they agree, only that they take this reflecting position relative to the dialogue. This allows us to perform for them, and, in the process of this performance, we can present them with many models of dialogue, such as discussion, disagreement, humour, etc. In the content of this performance, we can present many new options for their dilemma, as well as new ideas and perspectives about the dilemma.

Ivan: Sure. I'm wondering if Mom and Dad can be patient. Patience may be required about the form that Barbara will use to tell it. She may be exploring a whole new way of communicating. So we might have to be patient. Will you let us know when you cannot be patient any more (to parents)?

Ivan responds by trying to support the parents, while empowering Barbara. He is asking the parents to be patient with us, and implying that there will come a time when they will not be able to remain patient, and that they should let us know when that happens.

(Parents agree by both nodding their heads at the same time.)

Jeri: Barbara, in what way is Silvia handling it? Is it a new way for you? Is it the same as your Mom and Dad?

They agree to be patient, and thereby allow themselves to take a reflective position while remaining in contact with us.

(Barbara shakes her head no, indicating it is not the same)

It's different from your Mom and Dad. How is it different? Can you tell me?

Ivan: (To Jeri) Could you ask her, is it that she can't tell you or she won't tell you?

Ivan is supporting Jeri without getting in her way. He asks Jeri to ask Barbara, in order to not interfere, and thereby shows respect for their dialogue.

Jeri: Is it that you can't tell me or you won't tell me? Did you lose the words? Did you decide not to?

When we come to a dead end, we reframe the question, trying to make it a bit safer for Barbara to answer. By slowly

(She nods yes)

OK. You decided not to. If Mom were to tell me how the family is handling it with Silvia, would it be very different from what you would tell me?

Barbara: Probably.

Jeri: Probably. If Dad was to tell me how you and Silvia are handling this, would it be very different from what Mom would tell me?

Barbara: Maybe.

Jeri: And would it be very different from what you would tell me?

Barbara: Probably.

Jeri: And how about if Steven were telling me. Would it be different again?

Barbara: Most likely.

Jeri: So, most likely if everybody were to tell what is happening in the counseling, we'd have four different stories.

Barbara: Maybe.

expanding the question to include the rest of the family, we can allow her to know how they would feel and, thus, empower Barbara.

Jeri then proceeds with Barbara about the issue of how Silvia is "handling it." But this time she adds a new idea. Is Silvia handling it in a way that is new for Barbara? Perhaps this way is different from the way Mother and Father would handle it. Jeri is attempting to show the family that Silvia is using options other than confrontation, negative interpretation, embarrassment, and anger to work with Barbara.

Repeating the words, like, "would it be different if Steven were telling me," we create a serial conversation which helps the client to organize her thinking and create linkages in her ideas about the subject. This also slows down the pace of the conversation, giving her more time to think. And most importantly, by adding one member of the family at a time to the question, it allows us to look together at differences among family members and for the family members to reflect on what they hear from each other.

Jeri: And If we maybe have four different stories, which one of them would be more similar to yours?

Barbara: Probably Steven's.

Jeri: So he would see it more like you do.

Barbara: (Nods yes)

Jeri: And whose would be more like Mom's?

Barbara: Dad's.

While staying in the process of "how" and not "why," Jeri shifts from questions about differences to questions about similarities. Contrasting differences and similarities creates a context with new meanings and metaphors.

Jeri: Dad's would be more like Mom's. So they try to get their stories somewhat together. Are they a good team . . . a strong team?

Barbara: (tentatively shakes head yes)

Jeri: Pretty strong huh?

Barbara: Kind of.

Jeri: When are they the strongest?

Barbara: During discipline.

Jeri: And when are they not very strong?

(No response)

We have created the second shift. We have begun to look at some of the family process together. They have given up content for the moment, allowing us to establish differences and alliances.

How about you and Steven? Do you make a pretty good team with Steven?

(Steven turns to look at
   Barbara)

Barbara: Sometimes.

Jeri: Whose the pitcher?

Barbara: (Pointing to Steven)

Jeri: He's the pitcher. Does that
   mean you are the catcher?

Barbara: (Shakes head no)

Jeri: No. What does that mean
   about you?

Barbara: We're both pitchers.

Jeri is attempting a little humour with Barbara, as she tries to help differentiate her role from her brother's. Jeri creates the content of the metaphor, baseball; Barbara completes it with her own meta-meaning about being in a symmetrical position relative to her brother and relative to the parental team. Perhaps Barbara's response about her and Steven both being pitchers is her way of telling us that they are not really a team.

They are together by default, and are in competition with each other.

Jeri: That's an unusual team.
   Two pitchers.

(Silence)

   (Talking to Ivan) We have
   four different stories. Two of
   them seem more alike. Can
   we assume we have two
   teams?

At this point, we are beginning to see that Barbara and her brother are on one side and the parents are on the other side.

Ivan: (Taking the role of Steven)
   I'm sorry. I'm not here.

Jeri: Really!

Ivan: I'm on the floor (looking
   at Steven).

Ivan has become keenly aware of Steven's silence, and, in his attempt to maintain neutrality, he is trying to support and empower Steven. Ivan uses humour and seriousness in a delicate balance.

(Steven laughs and looks up at Ivan in the chair)

I'm him (meaning Steven).

Jeri: All right. How are you doing?

Ivan: I'm playing. I'm doing fine. I want you to know that I am listening very, very carefully.

Jeri: I'm glad.

Ivan: I understood everything you have said, but I'm not here. I'm worried though about my Mom and Dad.

Jeri: You are?

Ivan: Because I think they wanted something else here.

Jeri: Uh huh.

Ivan: I'm not here though.

Jeri: What do you think about that Steven? Does that sound silly?

Steven: (Shakes his head no)

Steven: (Then shakes his head yes)

"I'm not here" is an analogic form of inclusion with Steven and the literalization of a metaphoric action. Ivan uses it as a way of giving a voice to Steven while acting on a hunch about how to relieve the tension he perceived building in the parents as a result of restraining them from divulging Barbara's secret. Ivan acted on his impulse of anxiety about the parents by using the voice of Steven to convey concern.

By reflecting the fact that Steven is listening very carefully, Ivan reminds the family that, in his silence, Steven is playing out his role as a member of the family. Ivan is simultaneously able to convey his concern about the parents.

We shift into a different kind of teamwork that requires Jeri to be in complement with Steven in a way that Ivan cannot because he is now in symmetry with Steven. Ivan refers to his worry that the parents are not getting what they came for, and he expresses it through Steven. Jeri moves that idea along by asking Steven if he worries about his parents too.

Steven's spontaneous answer to Jeri is that it does not sound silly, but as he becomes self-

Jeri: Yes . . . Wait a minute. We have the signals mixed up here.

Mother: That's a yes.

Jeri: Yes. Does that sound silly to you. He's not really on the floor. Do you think that he might really be worried about your Mom and Dad? Do you worry about your Mom and Dad?

Steven: (Nods yes)

Jeri: Yeah! Anybody else worry about your Mom and Dad? Does your sister worry about your Mom and Dad?

Your sister does too. Huh. Somebody else too beside your sister? Aunts, uncles, cousins, grandparents?

Steven: (Nods yes)

Jeri: Everybody! Oh my gosh. That's a lot of worrying.

(Steven nods his head vigorously)

Ivan: Wouldn't you?

Jeri: Gosh, I don't know. I forgot to be worried. I even forgot to breathe.

Ivan: (Taking the role of Steven again) If you knew what I

conscious in the group he realizes that it must sound silly to them so he changes his answer to conform.

Jeri tries to mediate between the meta-levels that are in operation.

Jeri is reflecting the tremendous amount of tension in the family. By using her own felt tension "I forgot to breathe," Jeri is bridging the gap from metaphor to the reality experienced in the room.

Again Ivan is taking an enormous risk by brushing up

know but haven't told you, you would worry.

Jeri: Mmmm.

Ivan: (to Barbara) Do you worry about him? Does he (Steven) worry about you? So, you two are OK.

Jeri: Did you agree with your brother that other people worry about Mother and Father besides the two of you?

Barbara: (She nods yes)

Ivan: (To Mother) Is this a surprise to you?

Mother: No

Ivan: Do you accept the worry or do you fight against it?

Mother: I accept it.

Ivan: You accept it. How long have they worried?

Mother: Probably all their lives. Don't we all worry about our parents?

Ivan: I don't know. Did you worry about your parents?

Mother: Yeah! I worry about my Mom and how she's doing and stuff.

Ivan: And do you think your daughter worries about the same things that you worried

against the idea of secrets in the family.

Now we enter the process of differentiation. Making distinctions is a way of slowing down the amount of information as well sorting it.

Before going too far with this concept of worrying, it is important to find out whether it is all right with Mother to have all this worrying going on. Ivan offers complementary possibilities to Mother as a way of giving her options and not letting her feel stuck on one side of the issue. Asking a question in this way allows for a response at either polar end of the recursion or somewhere between.

Next Ivan amplifies worrying to include other generations, still offering complementary possibilities. By bringing in other generations, we are trying to help Mother and daughter see that they are part of a larger picture of how relationships are handled. Worrying is one about with your mother or different things?

Barbara: Different.

Ivan: Different?

Mother: I think in a lot of ways she worries about similar type things.

Ivan: Could you name one that you and Barbara have in common? That you worry about your mother and she (Barbara) worries about you?

Mother: (Looks at Barbara) Well, I was raised by a single parent and so my Mom was a person that got all the atten . . . got all my attention. But our relationship has been rocky at times. I see her (Barbara) trying to give me the type of strength and support I gave my mother.

Ivan: I'm not sure I got that. Will you say that again.

Mother: OK. The type of strength and support that I had given my Mother when she was alone is similar to the support Barbara gives to me when my husband and I have problems.

Ivan: As if you were alone?

vehicle of relationship between mothers and daughters in the family.

We try to help the Mother make distinctions between her worrying and Barbara's worrying. Mother sees her daughter worrying about her in ways that are similar to the ways in which she worried about her mother. However, Mother's mother was a single parent. Barbara has two parents. This is an important difference between them. On the other hand, Silvia told us that Barbara is fearful her parents will divorce.

Ivan attempts to help Mother distinguish between her worrying and Barbara's worrying. Mother seems unable to make the distinction, but she moves the conversation on with the word "support." Ivan picks up on the concept of support, after his initial confusion.

Mother makes a shift by positively connoting Barbara's behaviour. She is identifying with Barbara as a daughter who mothers her mother. Mother makes the comment that Barbara gives her support when she is having problems with her husband. It is as if, at those

Mother: As if I was alone.

Ivan: (To Father) What does that do to you?

Father: She gives me the same support.

Ivan: She does?

Mother: Uh huh.

Ivan: Wow.

Jeri: That's a lot of work.

Ivan: Two! You can support two at once! So, it's almost like you are the single Mother (to Barbara).

Barbara: (Hides her face)

(Pause)

Ivan: That's a tremendous job. How does she do it?

times, she is a single parent and Barbara can support her, as she supported her single-parent mother.

We are impressed with the amazing amount of support that Barbara can show, and we attempt to amplify that. Mother tells of Barbara's support, bringing it almost to the level of absurdity. We respond with equal intensity, pleased to be so positive, but aware that we have moved to the opposite position from where we started. Feeling like alchemists, we watch as Mother's negative attributions towards Barbara transform into positive attributions.

Ivan asks *how* does she do it (support both parents). If he were to ask *why*, it would move us into content, and we want to stay in process. Asking *how* maintains the conversation at the level of process. We will attempt to keep the dialogue at this extraordinary, positive level for some time. We will exclaim praises. Ivan does this by speaking what might seem to be the unspeakable, punctuating the fact that Father

Barbara: (Whispers something)

Father: She's whispering — hyper-energy.

Ivan: Do you think she has more energy than the two of you?

Mother and Father: (Simultaneously) Definitely.

Father: Definitely more than her Mother anyway.

Ivan: (To Father) Do you have energy like your daughter?

Father: Yes.

Ivan: So it runs in your family?

Father: No. I think I have even more than Barbara has because I require less sleep than she does too.

Ivan: So, you are up and ready to get support and she is still asleep.

Father: Uh huh.

Barbara: Huh uhh. (Shakes head no vigorously)

Ivan: Huh uhh. You mean you get up first to give him support and he's still asleep?

Barbara: No, but I go to bed late, and I get up late.

Father: Late!

Barbara: Late! (laughs with Father)

is really eager for Barbara's support.

Barbara brings in the idea that "hyper-energy" allows her to parent her parents. Going along with this, Ivan asks the parents whether she has more energy than they do.

Ivan continues the absurdity by asking Father if he is up and ready for support while Barbara is still sleeping. He speaks what might be thought of by some to be the unspeakable, punctuating the fact that Father is extraordinarily eager for his daughter's support.

Barbara and the Father joke about her going to bed late and getting up late, a subject that twenty minutes ago would have brought out some hostile

Ivan: Maybe that's what happens when you are supporting two people. You have to get a lot of sleep. But you have to stay up late to make sure they are OK. But you don't have to support your brother?

(Silence)

(to Jeri) I would like to go back to something.

Jeri: Oh! I was down on the floor.

Ivan: Oh! Do you want to stay there?

Jeri: No. It's all right. I'll come back.

Ivan: Thank you. I was wondering how it is that Mom and Dad have been able to let Barbara know what they need. How they do that . . .

Jeri: I was wondering whether Mom and Dad are alone in teaching Barbara or whether there are more people involved.

Ivan: So, somebody else outside of this immediate family could have taught her.

remarks from both of them. They seem to accept Ivan's conclusion that supporting two people is exhausting. Ivan is using the family's meaning system and attempting to have them hear the absurdity of what they are saying. When the parents have a problem, Barbara's role is to act as though each of them is a single parent. We do not need to know whether they have heard any of this. We hope to be seeding their thoughts for their own therapy later.

Jeri then moves in to Steven's position as a way of reassuring Steven and his family that he has not been all alone.

Here we reflect on their ideas. The family listens while we talk about ideas and check them out with each other.

It takes two of us to keep track of both the verbal and nonverbal responses in this family, and it helps when the two of us talk to each other and check out or reflect on what they are thinking and doing. When Jeri says, "No. It's all right. I'll come back," Ivan takes that as a signal that the tension is easing, and we can go on with the conversation. Jeri gives the "all clear" signal in

Jeri: I asked if there were more people and both children readily nodded their heads.

Ivan: We could find out who is missing.

(No response)

You probably have to suggest and then Steven will nod.

Mother: (To Steven) Do you remember the question?

Jeri: He hasn't missed a word ... I don't think. Could there be somebody missing ... an aunt ... an uncle ... a grandma ...?

(Steven nods yes after Barbara nods yes about Grandmother)

A Grandma !

Ivan: (Talking to Jeri who could not see that both parents had nodded yes about the missing Grandma). They (meaning both parents) agree, by the way.

Jeri: Thank you.

Ivan: Barbara agrees, it's Grandma.

Barbara: It's Nanna !

Jeri: Where is Nanna, Steven?

Steven: New York.

Jeri: Where in New York?

Barbara: (Goes over to Steven and whispers) Long Island.

metaphor, as if she were Steven.

Realizing that Steven has been left out of this process, Jeri brings him in gently.

Barbara is now cooperating. She is ensuring that the conversation will go on. Perhaps because it's something she wants to talk about. Both children agree about who is missing. It is our job as teammates to inform each other of

Jeri: Oh. Long Island. That's a long way away?

Steven: Pretty long.

Jeri: (to Barbara) Does that seem like a long way away to you?

Barbara: Not really.

Jeri: Not really. That's quite a country we have where 3,000 miles isn't very long.

Ivan: (Talking to Jeri) We have learned from AT&T not to accept distance calls. I wonder why they are so far away. If Nanna is so important, why are they so far away?

Jeri: (Talking to Ivan) Maybe it doesn't seem so far away. Maybe they see each other quite often.

Ivan: Like right around the corner.

Barbara: Every year.

Ivan: Whose mother is Nanna?

Mother: That's my mother.

Ivan: Your mother. Not yours (to Father).

Father: No. Nanna is her mother and Grandma is my mother.

anything that one of us may not have been aware of, and to incorporate that message in the interview as a reflecting process. It is when the subject of grandmother surfaces that both children become engaged in the interview.

Now Barbara is voluntarily in the conversation. She has come a long way from the child who initially refused to talk. She has maintained nonverbal contact throughout the interview, and she continues to do so with her eyes.

Both of us get into the rhythm of sharing the conversation and taking turns exploring a particular idea. As one of us talks, the other observes and tracks, and then, we switch. Often it takes two of us to track, amplify, expand, and reflect on a conversation in order to engage members of a family and not be confined to narrow one-on-one conversations with each family member.

We take time out to reflect with one another. This gives us time to re-group, make contact, and talk about the family in a way that the family is compelled to listen. This time allows for punctuating, reframing, and saying things to each other that

Barbara: Grandma is in Florida.

Jeri: I want to go back to what we were talking about. How Barbara may have learned to do this. I was suggesting maybe she didn't learn it in this immediate family ...

Barbara: Yes.

Jeri: That there was a larger family that included Nanna.

Ivan: (To Jeri) Does Nanna know about this embarrassment that Barbara doesn't want to talk about here? Is she a part of the family that Barbara gets to talk to about this thing that's private with Silvia?

Jeri: What? Is Nanna a part of the family that Barbara gets to talk to about the thing that's private between Silvia and Barbara? I don't know.

Ivan: See, the whole thing may be taken care of already with Silvia. That's what I'm wondering.

Jeri: I would assume that if Nanna worried and Barbara worried that Barbara and Nanna would worry together.

Barbara: (Shakes head no)

might be too confrontational to say to family members.

The issue of the secret is always there. Now we are trying to show the family that the issue can be dealt with as a process. We bring it up now to see if something has changed. We again flirt with danger, not for its own sake but to determine what is different, if anything, as a result of the conversation up to this point.

Jeri reintroduces the concept of worry and now recreates it as a recursive process with the larger family.

Jeri: No? OK. So, if you worry and Nanna worries, you worry separately?

Barbara: (Shakes head yes)

Jeri: OK. Separately.

Ivan: Does Nanna worry about you (to Barbara)?

Barbara: (Shakes head yes)

Jeri: Does Nanna worry about Steven too?

Barbara: (Shakes head yes)

Jeri: My goodness, there's a lot of worrying.

Ivan: (To Barbara) How about your Mother? Does she worry about her daughter? Does she worry about your Father?

Barbara: (Shakes head yes)

Ivan: Does she worry about the same things about everybody or different things?

Barbara: Different.

Silvia: (To Jeri) Does Mother talk to Nanna about her worries about Barbara ?

Jeri: (To Mother but is interrupted by Barbara's whisper) Do you talk to your Mother . . . about your daughter . . .

Ivan: (To Barbara) Then do you talk to Nanna about things

As we continue to amplify on the issue of worry, we are establishing the idea that worrying is a multi-generational activity — not a strange, isolated or pathological state in the family. It is a process some members of the family use to express feelings about and toward one another.

that you worry about, about
your Mother?

Barbara: (Shakes head no)

Ivan: You don't.

Jeri: Father, where do you fit
into this? Do you talk to her
mother too?

Father: Oh, yeah!

Jeri: You do.

Now that we have amplified
the situation, we are honing in
and differentiating worries in
almost rhythmic fashion. So far,
we see that there are differences
in who worries with whom and
about whom. At this point Jeri
wants to include Father who
seems left out of this dialogue
about worrying patterns that
exists among the women in the
family. The theme of secrets
and loyalty continues. We
learned from Silvia that Barbara
had asked her paternal
grandmother if she could come
live with her if her parents
divorced. Barbara tells us she
does not talk to her
grandmother about her Mother.
It might be disloyal to say she
relies on her grandmother,
especially as we are about to
hear that Mother does not talk
with her mother-in-law.

Mother: But, I don't talk to his
family.

Jeri: But you (Father) talk to
Nanna about things that
worry you .

Father: About the family.

We have now engaged all
members of this nuclear family
about the worrying and have
linked it to the previous
generation they left behind in
New York. All goes along well
until Mother stops the rhythm
by telling us she does not talk to

Jeri: (To Father) So you might talk to Nanna about Mother as well as Barbara?

Father: Uh huh.

Jeri: Does anybody ever hear these conversations you might have with Nanna?

Father: Sure, once in a while.

Jeri: (To Barbara) Does anybody ever hear conversations you might have with Nanna?

Barbara: uh . . .

Mother: Occasionally. Usually we call between work hours.

Barbara: (whispers) To Grammy . . .

Ivan: Your Mother said that she doesn't talk to your Fathers's parents. Do you?

Barbara: uh huh.

Ivan: Do you know her reasons for not talking to them?

Barbara: uh huh. Mommy doesn't like Grammy. And Grammy doesn't like Mommy.

her husband's family. She announces the rupture between her in-laws and herself.

The themes in this family seem to be secrets, worry, loyalty, and embarrassment. We press on in this uncertain conversation about the politics of the family, i.e., who talks to whom about what, and what are the consequences of these relationships.

Ivan goes back to an earlier moment when Mother said she does not talk to her Mother-in-law. He asks Barbara about this, which has the effect of pushing the parents into an observering and reflecting position as they listen to what Barbara thinks about the Mother's relationship with her Mother-in-law. Barbara is quite candid about the mutual dislike between the two women.

Ivan: Mutual?

(Pause)

What does that do to your Father?

Barbara: Nothing. It doesn't bother him.

Jeri: It doesn't bother him?

Barbara: No. It doesn't.

Father: It bothers me a little bit. But, no, I have my own relationship with my family and so . . . she's not friendly with her, then she's not friendly with her.

Ivan: Do you know the reasons why this has happened?

Father: Oh Yeah. It's been pretty much over the years. It's been going on about 15 years.

Ivan: But it doesn't affect you? Or does it affect you?

Father: I'm sure it affects me a little bit but not a whole lot.

Ivan: Do you think it affects your relationship?

Father: To some degree. To some degree that's why we came 3,000 miles away.

Ivan shifts to get Barbara's views on the effects on the Father of the rift between Mother and Grandmother.

Jeri joins in to reflect with Barbara on whether the rift between Mother and Grandmother bothers Father, which engages Father.

At this juncture in the interview we are in the "interior" of the extended family and have engaged the family in conversation about their interpretations (explanations, significations, and understandings) of the relationships among themselves, and between them and extended family members. This has taken us away from the initial conversation about Barbara as the problem of the family, and brought us to a conversation concerning continuity between this nuclear family and the Father's family of origin.

Ivan continues to explore how the rift between Mother and Mother-in-law affects others in the family. Father explains that the impact of the rift was responsible for the family's moving away from New York.

Ivan: To do what? I mean about the relationship. Your parents . . .

Mother: To keep them out of it.

Ivan: To keep them out of your relationship.

Jeri: And how effective has that been?

Mother: ummm. Pretty good. I've lived 150 miles away and they have just dropped in on me. 3,000 miles is more distance to drop.

Jeri: So when you lived in New York they just dropped in on you. And one of the effects of being here is not having the unpredictability of their dropping in? Are there any other effects of being 3,000 miles away as opposed to 150?

This family is now estranged from his family of origin and trying to function in isolation 3,000 miles away from home. The strain may be too great to allow them to effectively work out their conflicts with the extended family. This may put Barbara in the position of being the organizing link with the extended family. However, without their presence, Barbara may appear to be the symptom bearer of this nuclear unit of the extended family on both maternal and paternal sides of the family.

Jeri engages Mother in a conversation about "effectiveness," which implies a process as opposed to the content of the problems between Mother and her Mother-in-law. We are interested in the "how" or process questions. They focus on the relationships among people and their meanings rather than the content. As Jeri continues to talk with Mother about "effects" or process, Mother attempts to veer off into content, i.e., manipulations and negative attributes.

Mother: It's just that they haven't been able . . . they are very manipulative people . . . and that they haven't been able to manipulate me. I saw it with my brother-in-law and his first wife and how they were able to manipulate . . .

Jeri: You know I have been thinking Ivan . . . it really hit me hard . . . that the trade off for leaving the East Coast, leaving his parents, meant Mother also had to leave her mother.

Jeri, sensing this move toward content and attributions, stops the dialogue with Mother and turns to Ivan to slow things down and to reflect again on effects rather than contents or attributes. Mother may be paying a great price for the rift.

Mother: (Nods yes)

Barbara: (Whispers to Father) I have to go (to the bathroom).

Ivan: You might have to say this again (to Jeri), but right now she has to go to the bathroom. They both have to go to the bathroom.

We reflect on the effects of this family leaving their family of origin by including the grandparents in New York, and we move in the direction of co-creating meanings about this nuclear family in relation to the extended family. However, there is an abrupt break while the children leave the room for over five minutes. What a coincidence!

Mother: Just tell them the way.

Ivan: To the left. We will wait for you. We won't talk until you come back.

(Children leave)

Mother: One of the things that Silvia and I are going to start dealing with is . . .

Ivan: (Breaks in and stops Mother) I promised.

We have a critical moment in the interview. The two children

Mother: Really (laughs uncomfortably).

leave, and the parents intend to carry on the conversation in their absence. Parents often feel they do not have to respect their children's rights to be part of a conversation about them. It is at this point that the parents could conceivably divulge the secret. Then we would be compromised in our neutrality (multipartiality) and would also commit a common cultural act against children by talking to their parents and disregarding the rights of the children. We are not going to let that happen. It could cause a rift between us and the parents. Nonetheless, we take that chance and remain silent for over five minutes while the children go to the toilet.

Ivan: I have to be true to my promise. Otherwise things will get confused. I'm sorry. This is a hardship, I know. Waiting is tough.

During the silence, Ivan makes a statement of understanding to the Mother whom he believes the silence is hardest for. This may allow Mother to tolerate it longer.

Jeri: I'm sure as parents they must be used to it.

(Pause)

Then Jeri reinforces the waiting by positively connoting waiting as a known parental state.

Ivan: (to Mother) But, I hope you won't forget what you were about to say.

Mother: I won't.

Ivan reminds the Mother to hold onto her place. He promises continuity as the reward for patience.

(Silence prevails for over five minutes. Barbara returns first)

Jeri: Will your brother find his way back?

Barbara: Yeah.

(Silence again for two minutes while waiting for Steven)

(Mother directs Barbara to go find Steven. She leaves again. Another silence for a few minutes)

(Silence continues)

Mother: (Mother whispers to Father) Maybe you should go get them.

(He gets up and leaves to find the children)

Jeri: Some things you just can't rush.

Mother: You can't send a girl to the men's room either.

(The children return. Steven returns to his place on the floor)

Mother: (To Steven) Do you want to sit in the chair for a while?

Jeri: I remember what I was about to say. Do you remember what you were about to say?

Mother: I wanted to say that one of the things that Silvia and I are starting to work on

is the way Barbara and I deal
with my Mother-in-law...
She has always been able to
buy Barbara's affections and
to buy me out of them.

Ivan: (To Jeri) Excuse me.
Did you hear what Barbara
said ...

Jeri: No.

Barbara: I still love my
Grandma.

Mother: I'm not telling you not
to love your Grandma. I just
want you to see her for what
it really is.

Ivan: If you could tell her what
it really is, in a way she
could hear, do you know
how you would tell her?

Mother: mmmmm.

Ivan intervenes to stop Mother
who is getting agitated. He
wants Mother to hear Barbara's
feelings of love for her
Grandmother. Mother tries
again to convince Barbara of
Grandmother's negative
attributes. We try to move the
conversation into "how" their
relationship works rather than
the "what" of it not working.
Ivan tries to help Mother
approach Barbara in a way that
Barbara could hear. By asking
Mother to alter her approach to
Barbara, Mother might find a
new way that could incorporate
Barbara's perspective. This may

Ivan: But before you answer that, let's take a moment. Barbara, do you think there's a way Mother could say that to you that you could hear it?

Barbara: (makes a gesture, like a shrug)

Ivan: You're not sure? So maybe she should save it until you are sure? So it may be too early to ask that. What would you have to do to get ready for her to say it so that you could hear it? If your mother practiced saying it to you would it help?

Barbara: (shakes head no)

Ivan: That wouldn't help?

(To Mother) You might have to practice with somebody else.

help Mother observe her own actions and thinking.

We try to have Barbara help her Mother. This is a way to help in the recursive nature of their relationship. Mother can help Barbara hear, and Barbara can help Mother articulate it differently. It is a positive reframing of a negative relationship.

We also respect the problem of both the Mother's ability to articulate and the daughter's ability to receive information by using time as our question about readiness. Ivan is persistent and works carefully with both of them on this issue to tease out the nuances of their relationship with the paternal grandmother.

We introduce new concepts to Mother and daughter, concepts of how to use time in order to get ready to hear something, and practising how to say it. By offering new and different ideas, we introduce processing, moving forward through conversation without getting stuck in content, or holding together. Introducing processing has the effect of altering the meaning of heretofore static contents.

By involving Barbara and Father in Mother's dilemma

Who would you practice with? (Mother looks at Father) Could he hear this and help you practice?

Mother: (gestures toward Father) He's heard this before.

Ivan: How about saying it in a way that he and Barbara haven't heard. Is there a different way you could say it?

Mother: I could work on it.

Ivan: You could work on it. And is that what you and Silvia are working on or is it something different?

Silvia: We have just begun to talk about this dilemma.

Ivan: (to Silvia) Do you talk only with Mother or with Barbara also about this?

Silvia: Everyone.

Ivan: They are all together? When you are talking about it, what is Barbara doing?

Silvia: Well, she's usually getting more active as she was doing today. She was quiet when she came in today and she gets what I think is more uncomfortable as the subject comes up. She

about her Mother-in-law, and her Mother-in-law's relationship to Barbara, we hope to alleviate Mother's sense of loneliness in the dilemma. By involving the others, we move the dilemma to the relationship level and away from the content level. However, there seems some uncertainty about the possibility of alleviating Mother's isolation.

Out of concern for Mother's feelings of isolation, Ivan brings Silvia into the conversation. This expands the dialogue to include the process that develops when the family interacts about Grandmother and their views of her and issues with her.

Ivan helps the family listen to Silvia talk about Barbara's behaviour in a context that is different from the way they usually talk about her behaviour. We try to help the family hear Silvia's ideas about how painful this is for Barbara.

moves her feet a lot, wants to
go out of the room, or
distracts the family.

Ivan: Does that mean she has
accomplished what she
wanted, or does it backfire?

Silvia: Well, she pays a price.

Ivan: Do you think she is
willing to pay the price?

Silvia: Well, I think she . . . yes I
do.

Ivan: So, at least in your
presence she seems willing to
pay the price of being
disciplined for doing
something to get something
else to happen or not to
happen.

Silvia: Yes.

Jeri: Barbara, did you follow all
that? They said you pay a
price. I don't know what that
means. (Barbara nods no) Do
you? What do you think?

(Silence)

Mother: Could you please stop!
You have a tongue!

After a long silence, Mother
breaks in. As Mother hears
about Barbara paying a price
for expressing her anxiety, she
gets more angry. She attacks
Barbara with "Could you please
stop. You have a tongue!"

Ivan: I have a feeling I have to
go away first.

Jeri: Go away? What do you
mean go away?

Ivan takes the role of Steven to
voice alarm and the wish to
withdraw. This has the effect of
stopping the interaction. He

Ivan: I don't know what I mean. But I have a feeling I have to go away first. Before she can talk.

Jeri: Why is that?

Ivan: I can't tell you. I'm only 7. I don't know what else to tell you.

(Children start laughing)

Ivan: I just know I have to go away.

Jeri: Oh. That will leave me rather lonely won't it?

and Jeri dialogue about staying or leaving. By saying he has to go away first before Barbara can talk, Ivan is going with a hunch about the relationship between Mother, Barbara, and Steven. The hunch is that Mother and Barbara are in a symmetrical fight over Steven's place in their relationship. This is also what fuels the fight with Grandmother. Ivan's hunch is that it could also be over Barbara's jealousy of Steven and his relationship with Mother. This hunch is later confirmed when Mother relates that Barbara felt her life ended when Steven was born.

By becoming Steven again, Ivan takes the tension between Mother and Barbara and "holds" it. "In metaphor," we have a complementary conversation about being there or not, being partners and being lonely. This hearkens back to the conversation with Barbara about teams. The family may experience us as if we were Barbara and Steven, a metaphor in action. We give voice to the children so the parents listen. They hear unspoken thoughts about what the children might say if they used their reflective voices. Later, we positively connote the parents and children as responsible partners. We have begun to work on the hypothesis of role confusion in the family.

Ivan: I'm sorry, but I think you can handle it.

Jeri: I'm not convinced.

Ivan: You don't think you can handle it if I go away?

Jeri: Huh uhhh. No. You are supposed to be my partner.

Ivan is referring, in metaphor, to Barbara being able to handle "it." We are now in the flow of co-creating a metaphor in incomplete gestalts with the family and of transforming negative content into positive process. Once the new metaphor is being constructed we can weave in and out of the new context.

Ivan: So do you think the two of us should go to the bathroom now?

Jeri: Ummm. I don't think so.

Ivan: So we better stay.

Ivan: (To Jeri) You know, I'm impressed that the two parents don't leave. They don't even talk about leaving.

(Steven slips off the chair onto the floor to the left of Mother)

Jeri: They are very responsible people.

Ivan: So are the children.

Jeri: How is that?

Ivan: They know when to leave, when to stay, when to take care of their parents, and when not to.

We frequently use our "selves" while we take on the role of others in an "as if" state. We take a question (hypothesis) like "what would the children feel and what would they talk to each other about if . . ." We take what we think the other might be thinking and feeling, and in an act of inclusion, give it expression in a safe-enough way so that the family can listen and comment on it. These are our remarks about our interpretations of their intentions, and they may or may not fit the family's meanings. But it allows them to choose those words or ideas that do fit, and to let the rest go by.

Jeri: So, when Barbara and Steven leave it is a way of being responsible, leaving Mom and Dad to handle things?

Ivan: Maybe.

Jeri: That makes sense to me.

Ivan: (Taking the role of Steven) I'm gone. You can go ahead. If you want to.

Jeri: Without you?

Ivan: Oh sure. I'm just playing.

Jeri: I don't want to do that. He wants me to go on without him. Do you think he's missing you Steven?

Ivan: You can't talk to me if I'm not here (in the role of Steven).

Jeri: Well, that's too bad. I was kind of interested in talking to you.

Ivan: You would like me to come back?

Jeri: Uh huh.

Ivan: (to Steven) Is it OK if I come back?

Steven: (Nods yes)

Ivan: OK. I'll come back.

Jeri: Thank you. I was beginning to feel kind of anxious.

By asking Steven if he can come back, Ivan solidifies his alliance with Steven. Ivan was talking about his anxiety in the role of Steven, so the family might see that Steven goes away when he is anxious.

By introducing anxiety into the conversation in the role of Barbara, Jeri creates the image

Ivan: That's why I left.

Jeri: Cause I was getting anxious?

Ivan: No. Cause I was getting anxious. (To Mother) Do you have any idea what this means?

Mother: I'm trying to follow it.

Ivan: Can you help us figure out what all this seems to mean?

Mother: With him (Steven) trying not to pay attention?

Ivan: Yeah.

Mother: Barbara would take negative attention over no attention at all.

Ivan: You mean she would stay to get it? What about Steven?

Mother: He'd rather be doing his own thing right now . . .

Ivan: Like leaving? Like he's doing?

Mother: Yeah. He'd be more than comfortable just to leave and do his own thing rather than to have the attention.

Ivan: But she stays to get the negative attention?

Mother: Yes.

Barbara: (nods no)

of Barbara as a young girl trying to cope with anxiety too.

At an appropriate moment, we move back to content. We ask Mother if she has any idea about what this dialogue between the two of us means. This gives her the opportunity to shift from her previous beliefs to different ideas as she considers our metaphoric constructions We are aware that by transforming the family's overt content into a metaphoric dialogue, we can express the covert content as well.

Mother now tells us what the dialogue means to her. Her reflections involve comparisons of her two children and their need for attention and how they manifest those needs. Mother's response represents a shift from the idea that Barbara is the problem, to the idea that Barbara would prefer to experience anxiety in the context of negative attention than to experience aloneness or isolation. Steven, on the other hand, from Mother's point of view, would rather have no attention than negative attention. He might prefer to escape anxiety in favour of aloneness or isolation.

Ivan: She's saying no about this. Father, what do you think? Could you help us make sense out of this thing?

Father: Yes. She likes to get the negative attention.

Ivan: What do you mean, "likes to?"

Father: There are times she will go out of her way to get the negative attention. She will argue a point until it is beyond reason and continue arguing even when she knows there is a consequence attached to it.

Jeri: Ivan. I don't know if you noticed but Barbara is shaking her head. She's not agreeing that she likes it.

Ivan: Huh. Did you know that she says she doesn't like it?

Father: I'm sure.

Mother: But she brings it onto herself all the time.

Jeri: Wait a minute. Wait. Wait. I'm getting confused. You said she likes it but then you said you are sure she doesn't. I'm confused.

Father: She does like the negative attention but she doesn't agree that she likes the negative attention.

Ivan brings Father into the conversation just as he did previously with Mother. Father seems to confirm what Mother said, and it furthers the hypothesis about Barbara's anxiety. We hope this represents a transformation in their thinking about their daughter.

During this sequence Jeri attempts to point out to the parents that Barbara is disagreeing with their view of her intentions.

The parents do not acknowledge this remark, so Jeri breaks in with her confusion as a way to amplify the absurdity of the dialogue, in the hopes that the parents will see that their interpretations of what they believe and Barbara's intentions do not fit.

Jeri: So you know what
  she likes and she doesn't
  know . . .

Father: At times.

Mother: She just wants the
  attention and it doesn't
  matter if it's good attention
  or bad attention, as long as
  it's attention.

Ivan: How does that tie in then
  with her supporting the two
  of you?

Ivan moves the conversation to
another level that can bring
together the two concepts of
Barbara's need for negative
attention and her need to be
responsible for both her
parents. We end that sequence
of dialogue because to continue
would be to further question
Father's authority, which
already seems tenuous and
ambiguous.

Mother: Because when there's
  distance between us (the
  parents), she comes in with
  her attention.

Ivan: But it's negative
  attention?

Mother: Well, no. In this case it
  could be positive attention.

Ivan: So, it could be positive?
  So she knows how to get
  positive attention too?

Mother: Mmm huh
  (confirmingly).

Barbara's behaviour relates to
her concern about the
possibility of her parents'
breaking up. She "comes in" in
the same way that her Mother
attended to the maternal
grandmother who was a single
parent, as we observed
previously.

Jeri: But, if she's supporting the
  two of you by taking on the

We push Mother into taking on
the struggle of how this concept

attention, why does she worry about you?

Mother: I think she worries about what effect it will have on me.

Jeri: I don't understand.

(Steven goes over to Barbara and sits on her lap)

Mother: Our relationship (Mother and Father) has problems and when there are problems between Father and I and we are apart, she comes in with a loving relationship and her love gets a positive attention.

Jeri: OK.

(Barbara plays Pat-a-Cake with Steven on her lap. Steven is sitting on her lap facing away from Barbara)

Mother: That's where the positiveness is . . .

Jeri: OK.

Mother: Now you want to know about the negative?

Ivan: (to Jeri) Well, could it be that negative is when the parents are together?

of worry fits into the recently established hypothesis of support and attention.

We now have several ideas in the weave. One is worrying, which came up previously in the conversation around the idea of supporting both parents as though they were single parents.

At this point, we find that Mother has made a shift by acknowledging that there are other ways to interpret Barbara's behaviour. She states that Barbara can and does elicit positive attention. Yet, in this statement, she again reveals that there are problems between herself and her husband.

As we move the conversation to another level, Mother responds with a comment that reflects the synthesis of the three ideas discussed. Mother indicates that when she and Father have problems, Barbara is loving and elicits positive attention from whichever parent she is attending to at the time. On the other hand, she elicits negative attention when the parents are together. There may be a precedent in the family for how the female child can elicit

Mother: Right. And it's been interesting . . . She's gone to camp twice this summer. One week when she was gone we got along quite well until the day before she got home . . .

Ivan: You and Father got along quite well?

Mother: Right. And then it was really craziness afterwards. She has just recently returned from camp . . . I laid a lot of laws down even before we got out of the airport . . . Things have been pretty smooth the last couple of weeks.

Ivan: You laid down the law.

Mother: Uh huh.

Barbara: (whispering) Mommy.

Father: There was also a lot going on when she came home the first time. We do a lot of charity work . . .

Jeri: So when the two of you are close together then Barbara comes along and comes between you . . .

Mother: Barbara has come out and told us she can only love one person at a time.

Jeri: And where would she have learned that?

Mother: Remember that Silvia? We talked about it.

positive attention when the parents are together. To complete this hypothesis in a circular fashion, it could be that Barbara finds ways to have her behaviour interpreted negatively so that the parents would be forced to be together. We have experienced this to be a common phenomenon in families where the parents are in serious conflict.

Mother continues to enhance and embellish the hypothesis that Barbara, as a third person, elicits negative attention by indicating that Barbara says that she "can only love one person at a time." We took this

Barbara: (continues whispering) Mom . . .

Mother: So it's that . . .

Barbara: (whispering) Mom. . .

Jeri: Where might that have come from?

Mother: Well, she feels like her life ended when her brother was born. She was six. She doesn't believe that I still loved her when he was born. That I could love him too.

to also indicate the reciprocal, namely that Barbara believes she can only be loved by one person at a time. That may be why she seems to only arouse negative attention when the parents are together.

Mother's comments that Barbara believes she can only love one person at a time and feels her life ended when Steven was born, contradicts what we see happening now. Steven is cosily sitting on Barbara's lap playing Pat-a-Cake, a game played between a mother and young child. Barbara is holding Steven as if he is a small child. Could it be that, as she sees this scene, Mother reflects about her own difficulties in loving both children at the same time? Does this reflect her own experience with her Mother?

Jeri: Oh. It's going too fast.

Jeri's words, "It's going too fast," alerted us to the fact that Mother was no longer integrating these ideas, but she was back to her negative attributions about Barbara.

Ivan: Wait. You're going too fast. I can't absorb all this so fast. See you've been through this experience and we're just trying to catch up. And what's really confusing me is she's (Barbara) got him

Ivan also intervenes with the need to slow down. He attempts to explain this to the family, that as consultants, we are just trying to understand and not just interrupting.

(Steven) on her lap. If her life ended at six when he was born . . .

Father: I can't believe the last time she had him on her . . .

Mother: . . . lap. Yeah!

Ivan: So something is changing here.

Mother: She's trying to show you a different side of her right now.

Ivan: Or maybe showing you.

Mother: Yeah (hesitatingly).

Ivan: What do you think about this new side that she's showing you?

Mother: Oh, I like when she gets along with her brother. It makes it easier to live at home.

Ivan: Do you think you can handle this . . . away from here I mean?

Mother: Yeah (hesitatingly)

Jeri: (concerning Steven) He likes it too.

Ivan: He likes it. How about you (Father)? You like it too?

Father: I like it.

Ivan: So, her life is beginning again.

Father: It's actually been pretty quiet since she came back from camp this last time.

Ivan points out that something is changing. Mother tries to attribute the change (of Steven on Barbara's lap) to our presence. Ivan confirms that the parents are still the most important people in Barbara's life, and that the change is for them. He asks Mother directly about this change in order to encourage her to respond positively in front of Barbara. Ivan then helps Mother to reassure Barbara that she can "handle" this positive change and more.

In the spirit of co-evolution, Ivan updates Mother's hypothesis about Barbara's life ending at six years of age when Steven was born. Ivan takes

Jeri: How does she know when you like it?

Mother: She's told that when she's doing something positive that it is positive.

Father: We try and express it to her.

Jeri: How do you express it?

Father: Tell her.

Jeri: What words would you use perhaps?

Mother: (Mother tells children they are getting too silly. Barbara is bouncing Steven up and down on her lap) I think you are getting too silly.

Father: Tell her that I'm noticing a change. That I like the change. That it's nice to see her making a change.

Ivan: (To Jeri — quietly commenting on what Barbara is doing with Steven in her lap) It's like she's playing pat-a-cake with a new born baby. It's wonderful. And he's willing. Maybe they've never seen this before.

Mother: He always wants attention.

Ivan: But this is the first time she has been willing to give it to him?

Barbara's play with Steven and amplifies it into something momentous. By saying that Barbara's life is beginning again, Ivan transforms the negative connotation Mother previously gave to Barbara's anxiety and creates the possibility that Barbara has changed.

Jeri presses for details of how they go about expressing positive regard.

Mother: Actually, since she's been home from camp. She's been gone for the last two weeks.

Barbara: Pretty much two weeks.

Mother: Yeah. So . . . it's a new thing. He hasn't gotten on her nerves yet or anything like that.

Jeri: And how would you show her if you were appreciating the change?

Mother: Actually, she and I have made major leaps since she's been home. I've seen growth in her and I've given . . . she's wearing make-up . . . something that hasn't been in the past . . .

Ivan: Sorry to interrupt, but you just said something, and she was trying to look at you, 'cause maybe she has never heard this. Could you look at her and tell her this? This may be something she has never heard. Barbara.

Barbara: What?

Ivan: Barbara, would you be willing to look at your Mother while she tries to tell you this?

Mother: It's that I felt that she has made efforts and in

This is a real turning point. Mother is becoming very positive about the recent changes Barbara has been demonstrating. We interpret Mother's shift as her response to the reframing and the positive connoting that we have been doing up to this point. It is a surprise to hear positive regard from Mother toward Barbara.

Jeri helps Mother with the idea of demonstrating or highlighting her appreciation of the changes Barbara exhibits. This is similar to our previous attempts at suggesting to Mother that she can find new ways to talk with Barbara and have positive effects on how they relate to each other.

At this point we encourage eye contact when Mother is talking to Barbara. Eye contact between persons in dialogue is one way to enhance the emotional contact they make when they talk. It is a way of trying to synthesize the verbal with the analogic aspects of conversation. To make eye contact is to enter into a form of emotional consensus, a sort of bonding about what was said at the verbal level. It confirms that the information has been received and that both the return that I am giving some more responsibilities to her that she has wanted.

Ivan: Wait . . .

Mother: (to Steven) Could you sit over here.

(Steven goes back to sit on the floor next to mother)

Ivan: (To Barbara) Can you tell your Mother what you heard her say? Could you look at her when you tell her this?

(Barbara nods yes)

Ivan: I know that's hard for you.

(Barbara starts to talk without looking at mother)

Wait, wait . . . You're not looking at her.

Barbara: (Glances at Mother) She said that I'm making progress . . .

Ivan: Wait. Excuse me. You're still not looking. You have to look at her.

Barbara: That I'm making good progress . . .

Mother: You're still not looking at me.

Barbara: (laughs) Making good progress and . . .

(Barbara talks softly so no one can hear)

words and the emotions have been "taken in." This cannot be attempted before we are accepted or included as trustworthy by the family and the co-created metaphor is sufficiently in the process of being established.

Mother has now taken over the initiative to make this kind of emotional contact with her daughter. Mother's actions reinforce her intentions to relate differently to Barbara. Barbara responds accordingly.

Ivan: (to Mother) Did you hear that?

(To Barbara) Do you think she heard you?

Mother: I think she heard as much of it as she wanted to hear.

Ivan: And how much do you think she heard of what you said?

Mother: That she's getting what she wants.

Ivan: Wait. Wait . . . you have to look at her.

Mother: (looking at Barbara) That you are getting what you want. I don't think you heard the part about what I want.

Stop (to Barbara).

Jeri: How could you make her hear it a different way?

Mother: (joking) Tie her up and knock her upside the head so you could keep her here.

Jeri: I know I used the word make. I meant how could you help her hear in a different way?

Mother: As she's doing things to let her know at the time that it's what I want out of her.

Jeri: Did looking at each other help at all?

This is an example of the need to use words carefully. To choose a word is to make a particular distinction, which invites a particular response or distinction that fits the word used. In this case, Jeri uses the word "make" which implies to the Mother that Jeri's intention is to have the Mother tell her how she might do it authoritatively. Mother turns this perceived demand into a joke. Perhaps she knows that it was not Jeri's intention, but she still has some angry feelings

Mother: Yeah. When you have eye contact, you know the person's hearing you.

Silvia: I had a fantasy of Mom sitting on Barbara's lap.

Jeri: Oh, you did?

Barbara: (laughs)

Jeri: Do you think Barbara could teach her the same thing (referring to Pat-a-Cake)?

Silvia: Maybe. I don't know.

Ivan: What about the other way around too? I was wondering when the last time was that Barbara sat on her Mom's lap.

Silvia: Right. I was thinking that too, but I thought it might be easier in the beginning for Mom to sit on Barbara's lap. Just for fun.

Mother: I won't break her legs (laughs).

Ivan: Sounds like you're even willing.

Mother: Yes (she says quietly)

Ivan: Did you hear that Barbara?

Barbara: Yeah. She said she wouldn't break my legs.

towards her daughter. Humour is a middle of the road response between her thoughts about Jeri's intentions and her feelings of anger about her daughter. Jeri then tries to clarify what she intended.

Silvia breaks in with a surprising and seemingly absurd idea. Mother likes the idea of sitting on Barbara's lap. This furthers the hypothesis of the role confusion in the family.

Ivan: What do you think about your mother sitting on your lap?

Barbara: She's too fat.

Ivan: She's too fat. Anything else?

Barbara: No.

Ivan: Then what would your father do if your mother was on your lap?

Barbara: Laugh

Ivan: He'd laugh.

He wouldn't be jealous?

Barbara: No. He'd probably try to sit on my Mom's lap and squish me.

Ivan: (to Mother) She takes very good care of you.

Mother: I know. She is a wonderful mother (laughs)

Jeri: But does she let you mother her?

Mother: Very little.

Father: She tries to do that.

Mother: She tries to be the mother in the house. Even when he was a baby, when it came to changing diapers and feeding and that stuff.

Ivan: So she thought when he was born that she was . . .

Mother: (breaks in) . . . the mother. She was the mother.

Mother previously stated that Barbara's life ended when Steven was born. We speculated that perhaps she meant Barbara's life as a child ended then. Now she tells us that Barbara became a "mother in the house" when Steven was born, an interesting transformation of ideas. Both

Ivan: (to Barbara) Do you remember that?

Barbara: (nods yes) Uh huh. I used to wake him up from his naps.

Ivan: Do you remember the moment you realized that?

Barbara: No.

Ivan: It just happened?

Barbara: Yep.

Ivan: So you haven't sat on her lap since then?

Mother: She has.

Ivan: She has.

Barbara: It's a hassle.

Ivan: When was the last time.

Barbara: At least two years ago.

Ivan: Two years.

Barbara: At least. Cause Mom says I'm too heavy to pick up, and I'm too fat to sit on her.

Ivan: She says you're too fat? And you say she's too fat.

Barbara: She doesn't say fat. She says too heavy.

Ivan: Heavy.

Jeri: Father. What does all that mean to you? All this talk about sitting on laps.

Father: I think that's kind of the way Mother expresses

Barbara and Mother confirm Barbara's surrogate motherhood. The implication is that Barbara mothers her own Mother as well as Steven.

The comment that Barbara is too heavy for Mother's lap suggests a metaphor that Barbara has grown up, possibly against her own wishes.

The last sequence synthesizes the interview through the dialogue about lap sitting. It seems that lap sitting is an apt metaphoric statement about this family. The exchange about laps and lap sitting, and the interchangeability about who sits on whose lap, represents to us comments about role changeability and possible role confusion. We have come a herself as far as maternal feelings of warmth.

Jeri: How she expresses herself. What is how she expresses herself?

Father: Sitting on her lap.

Jeri: Sitting on . . .

Father: . . . her lap

Jeri: Who is sitting on whose lap? I got lost.

Father: Either one.

Jeri: Either one of the kids sitting on Mom's lap? That's how Mother expresses herself? Do you get a way? Do you get a way in?

(Steven has moved on the floor between Father and Barbara)

Father: Yeah.

Jeri: You have a way in?

Father: Oh yeah. They come sit on my lap too.

Jeri: Who can sit on your lap?

Father: They both can. He comes on more than she does.

Ivan: How about Mother?

Father: She comes and sits on my lap sometimes.

Ivan: (to Mother) Do you get enough?

Mother: Not as much as I'd like.

Ivan: You'd like more.

great distance from the beginning of the interview when the parents arrived with a basket full of negative attributions about their children. We see them about to leave with their basket filled with positive attributions about Barbara and her relationship to her brother, her willingness to take on caring and responsibility for her parents, when they are in trouble, their willingness to allow her to be playful, and their acknowledgment that she has demonstrated major changes since returning from camp.

Jeri: That's funny. I had the feeling that Father would like more. I was watching his face and he's kind of getting left out of the lap stuff.

Ivan: What about Barbara?

Mother: She claims she never had it at all as a child so . . .

Jeri: So she never had it at all.

Mother: No.

Father: I'm surprised. She usually thinks its beneath her dignity.

Ivan: She has a lot of dignity here. You have already said that.

Mother: She was a queen. She was the only grandchild until he came.

Ivan: Whose queen?

Mother: Queen Barbara.

Barbara: (indicates quietly that she still is) I still am.

Ivan: She still is.

Mother: And up until recently . . .

Ivan: And did you have a king?

Mother: . . . and up until recently she's been the only girl too.

Barbara: I still am.

Ivan: She still is. What do you mean up until recently and she says I still am?

Mother: My brother-in-law just adopted a little girl.

Ivan: (to Barbara) Does she count for you?

Barbara: (shakes her head no)

Ivan: It doesn't count.

Barbara: He's not my uncle.

Ivan: He's not your uncle.

Father: Yes he is. She's mad at her uncle.

Ivan: You have disowned him?

Barbara: Yes.

Ivan: Queens can do that!

Barbara: uh huh. He was a bad uncle.

Ivan: What if they go wrong . . . with the family. Can you disown them . . . the rest of the family, if they go wrong.

Barbara: No. He did something very mean.

Ivan: He did. To you?

Barbara: Uh huh. Do you want to know?

Jeri: (Breaks in) Ivan. I wanted to caution you at this point. I think that there are lots of things that people have in this family that have been embarrassing and I think that they have been very clear that Silvia has been handling that content very well.

After all this conversation in which we worked to protect Barbara from embarrassing secrets, she teases us with yet another family secret. This one is about her uncle. It takes two of us to resist the attraction, but we are successful at protecting the family and their therapist so that together they can go on with their work.

Barbara: (whispering) He was a bad uncle . . . off with his head.

Ivan: OK. That's good enough for me.

Barbara: Do you want to hear?

Ivan: No. I don't.

Barbara: Please . . .

Ivan: It seems private. You have convinced me of the importance of your privacy. So I want to respect that all the time.

Barbara: (continues to whisper inaudibly)

Ivan: But thank you for asking me. I appreciate that. I think we are going to take a break now. It will be 15 minutes or so. Then we will come back and invite you in for about 5 minutes.

(Steven ends the session on the floor in front of his Mother)

We end the interview and begin the preparation for reflecting on our experience with the family. We do that by having each team member tell the therapist about their impressions or reactions to the family. The therapist then listens and determines what to share with the family during the postsession exchange with the family. Sometimes the therapist delivers all the reflections and, at other times, invites the consultants to say a few words to the family about their impressions. This is decided during the intersession discussion with the team.

Intersession discussion
with the team

Jeri: If you could say one thing to the family what would it be?

Ivan: Remember, this is a consultation, so our job is to help Silvia.

Sandra: I'm impressed with the amount of worrying that goes on in the family. I have some curiosity about what the family members worry about and about Mother's comment, "Don't all children worry about their parents?"

Eddi: I was struck by the fact that each person seems to need or want more lap sitting.

Robert: Metaphorically speaking, I am curious about how much lap sitting there is between Mother and Father.

Silvia: I thought it was brave of them to talk about their worrying here.

George: I'm concerned about Father getting lost or overwhelmed in the family.

Ivan: Silvia, there are two things I am very taken with about this family. One is the depth of their synchrony. They are in tune with one another at many levels, simultaneously. I am impressed about the level of comfort these parents have in being children and the comfort that the children have in being parent-like. As they presented it here, it's a complementarity I have not seen before without a great deal of anxiety. Mother may say she has some minor objections, but if you read their body language, they looked very comfortable with these ideas. It may end up being dysfunctional out in the world, but not in this context. It did not feel that way to me. I don't know what to make of it or how to put it in a couple of sentences.

Jeri: I am struck by the matrilineal legacy of the women. The maternal grandmother lost a father and probably was very young when she became a mother. The grandmother passed on the legacy to the daughters who evidently also married young and became mothers. This Mother was also super responsible, which she has clearly passed on to her daughter, Barbara. Somewhere in there is the thorn of only loving one person at a time. My hunch is that this is where the heart of the work is; in only being able to love one person at a time. Somehow, when the daughter, Barbara, was six and Steven was born, Barbara, began to transfer her love from Mother to Steven . . . but only could love one of them at a time.

Silvia: Mother identified that too. And Barbara talked about the other three, Mother, Father and Steven, being able to love more than one person at a time. It is only Barbara who cannot.

Ivan: That is part of the legacy Jeri is talking about. It does not get passed on to everybody. It gets passed on to one person — the queen.

Jeri: I am not sure that the other three family members can love more than one person. Perhaps Mother loved Father, and when Barbara came along she loved her, and when Steven came along she loved him.

Sandra: That fits with the description they gave that when Mother and Father are together, Barbara has to get the negative attention. So there is some message going back and forth about loving one person at a time from the parents too.

Ivan: There is another part of the message for me, which is that they have given the team a lot to think about. They came, in large part, to be helpful. I want to let them know they have been helpful by stimulating a lot of thinking at many levels. We will be sorting this out for a long time.

Eddi: I am struck by the skill that Barbara and Steven had in communicating nonverbally.

Jeri: (to Ivan) I think that last piece you and I could give to the family.

Silvia: I was going to say that Ivan can give the piece about synchrony and you, Jeri, the piece about the matrilineal relationship.

Ivan: Then the final thought goes with it. The one about having given us much to think about.

(Jeri agrees)

Jeri: How much do we want to say about the matrilineal legacy? Several things got passed down from grandmother to Mother to daughter. One of which was how to be such a good mother but another was to only be able to love one person at a time.

Sandra: I have a question about that. We think we know this is the case on the maternal side, but I would not rule it out on the paternal side. Father's mother does not seem to be able to love Mother. Is it based on their relationship or is it based on being able to love only one person at a time?

Silvia: Right. So I would pose it as a question. Did that message get passed down on both sides of the family?

Ivan: You can see it in this nuclear family when they talk about Barbara moving in as nurturer with one at a time.

Silvia: (cuts in) One question we might ask Barbara is, "Do you become disloyal if you love more than one person at a time?"

Jeri: uh huh. Which could create a disloyalty. OK, Let's try it.

Sandra: We don't know what that is about.

Jeri: No, but we could just say there is a possibility of that creating some concerns about disloyalty.

Jeri: (To the team) Thank you.

Message to the family

(B)arbara enters the room and asks Ivan and Jeri to close their eyes as she comes in the room)

Barbara: Open.

Ivan: Wow!

Jeri: Lovely.

(Barbara had picked some flowers and put them in a cup. She brought them as a gift and put them on the table.) Did you pick them just to match my dress? (To Steven) Did you come in with a treasure too?

Mother: He picked some flowers.

Ivan: So did Barbara.

Jeri: Did you see them?

Mother: Sure hope the church does not mind.

Silvia: We met with members of our team, and they gave me some impressions they would like for me to share with you. Then

Ivan and Jeri have something they want to share with you. One of the strong impressions I have is about how each of you do so much worrying about each other. There is a lot of worrying in the family. I also have the impression that each person in the family needs to or would like to have more lap sitting. And some members of our team were also worried and concerned about you, Father, and wondered if you were getting lost or overlooked.

Father: Hadn't thought about it.

Ivan: One of the things we were very impressed with is the depth with which all of you understand one another. Whether it is with words or in some other form. Whether you are seven, thirteen or adult, you seem to have a great depth of communication with each other. We were also taken with the observation that it seemed rare that parents could be so comfortable in the role of child with their children and how the reverse, that the children could be so comfortable in the role of their parents, seems also true. The children take comfort in being children and they seem to offer comfort in being parent-like. That is remarkable.

Mother: We also have a role model in the house where Dad does dishes and Mom works on the car.

Ivan: You have multiple roles . . .

Mother: We do.

Ivan: And you all seem comfortable with them.

Silvia: The nonverbal communication . . . Mother remarked to me how quiet both children were. I said we had noticed how they were communicating nonverbally during the entire time.

Jeri: (To Mother) I was impressed with the legacy that has been handed down from Mother to Mother on your side of the family. Being mothers early and being such good mothers. So nurturing and caring. I was wondering about the part you mentioned about Mother's being able to love only one person at a time . . .

Mother: uh huh.

Jeri: . . . and whether that was something that has been handed down by both sides of the family or just one. In my thinking about that, it made me wonder if there were aspects of disloyalty that went along with that. If you only love one person are you being disloyal to another? That is just some of the musings we have had. We just wanted to share with you. We hope it will be helpful to you.

Ivan: We want to thank you for your sharing. You have given us a considerable amount to think about, to mull over in our minds. We are full of ideas that you have presented to us. Is there anything you would like to share with us. Anything that might be of concern to you?

Jeri: Questions you have for us?

Father: Steven?

(No questions)

Ivan: With that we will stop. Thank you for coming.

Debriefing/reflecting

At this time, the entire Exchange Seminar group assembled to discuss their impressions of the interview. What follows is the conversation that ensued after the interview, inter-session and the delivery of the message to the family.

(The following persons from the exchange group all worked with us during the simulation, the interview, the creation of the message to the family and the debriefing.)

Ivan: Can we focus more on the process than the content of the interview? This is a training about the process and content of conducting an interview.

Jeri: You want to focus on process? It took a tremendous amount of discipline for me to focus on process and not the daughter, Barbara. She was the epitome of my friend in 5th grade. We went to the same camp and played the same hand game that Barbara was playing throughout the interview. It is a song. I thought this is my friend reincarnated. My friend annoyed her mother in similar ways. I was using all the discipline I could muster to stay in the present.

Ivan: In your feedback could you think about incorporating the experience of the simulation with the experience of the interview in your observations of the process?

Marti: I am interested in how you used the opportunity for them not to tell the secret.

Mary: I focused on leaving and feeling left.

Ivan: The simulation helped me take a leap of conceptualization and action. It gave me permission to actually perform the function of identifying and being inclusive with each of the children in their not wanting to be here. So I could talk out loud, as if I were one of them. I could not have done that without preparation. The children understood and accepted that process.

Marcia: Did the way Robert played Steven in the simulation give you a better sense of how to relate to Steven?

Jeri: Definitely.

Teri: They (the simulator and Steven) played with toys the same way.

Paddy: If you had not had the simulation and had not had that piece about the little boy, and if he had arrived quietly and sat underneath the table and stayed there during the entire duration of the interview, do you feel that it would have made any difference?

Jeri: Yes. It would have made a big difference. It would have felt terrible to me, and I would not have had a hypothesis about his sitting there. He is an important member of the family, and he did make a difference in his actions, if not by his words.

Ivan: I think that simulations are hypotheses-in-depth and in action. Without them I have to guess a lot at the abstract level. They translate abstraction into possible action. If I had been in an action, I can now do the reverse as well. I can't do the reverse as easily if I haven't had an action. The action can be very different. It does not matter what the action is. I do not care if the simulation actually simulates, reflects, or is in symmetry to what happens in the actual interview. What matters to me is that I have had an experience of action and an experience of abstraction and now can work at both levels simultaneously.

David: It puts you in an observer's position to your own therapy. You have sort of seen yourself doing the therapy. Now you can "see" it more from a systemic view.

Ivan: That allows me to take more risks.

Jeri: It allows us to practice where some of the pitfalls might be. It is like knowing where to navigate a bit more. The constructivists tell us that we navigate through life by a process of successfully or unsuccessfully missing rocks in the stream of life. Simulations give you practice at learning about some possible rocks to avoid. They do not tell you everything though. There are always more rocks, especially hidden ones. For Silvia it must have made a big difference not to have said anything about the Grandmother.

Silvia: Yes. I learned that in the simulation from feedback from Eddi (who played the Mother in the simulation).

Eddi: I thought that not continuing to talk when the children went to the bathroom gave a powerful message to the parents. What was going on when Ivan said he "wasn't there?"

Jeri: He was picking up on Steven. When I realized what was going on, I realized that Barbara was getting more anxious. As Steven was becoming more isolated, she was losing her partner.

Eddi: Jeri were you getting anxious?

Jeri: No.

Ivan: I understood that.

Jeri: As soon as I understood he was being inclusive with the boy, I realized I had a complementary role to play.

Doug P: You joined the family through the children.

Jeri: Sometimes it is easier that way . . . We do not always join a family through the children. But when I realized what Mother was up to, that she was on the brink of letting her negative feelings about her daughter splat all over, I knew we could be in for a difficult time. Had she been allowed to do that, we would have lost the children's trust, and it would have been difficult to get them in the conversation.

Ivan: One hypothesis I had was that the daughter acts out in response to the Mother's negative splats about her. Mother splats and acts like a child, and the daughter has to respond by doing something responsible. What do 13-year-olds do? They organize parents in a way that gets, as they put it, negative attention. But the negative attention forces the parents into being parents. When they come together as parents, Barbara loses her individual place with each of them.

Jeri: That was the only anxious moment I had, when I realized Mother was on the brink of doing that. If something didn't happen fast, it would have been a very difficult session.

Teri: When was that?

Jeri: When I made the mistake of asking them about their work with Silvia and what brought them in. I asked Barbara . . . and was I in trouble.

Ivan: That's when I left.

Jeri: He rescued me by distracting. Mother was right there on the divingboard . . . at the edge . . . about to lose her balance. Mother's splatting was going to be about Barbara and how bad she was and what she does wrong. She was pushed to another level and began talking about her Mother, which was important.

Eddi: In the simulation, as the Mother, that is exactly what I tried to do so I could control the situation. You did not allow that to happen in this experience.

Jeri: Right.

Karen: I wonder where you got the courage to stay with that girl so long because she was so uncomfortable.

Ivan: Any time I experience somebody with passion, I can connect with them. That is how it was relatively easy to stay with her.

Jeri: That's true. She was very passionate. Her eyes . . . I wish you could have seen her eyes.

Kathleen: So you didn't experience her as uncomfortable in a stay away from me posture?

Ivan: She was in a game . . . a passionate game. It was as if she said, nonverbally, "OK, let's play." I did not know how it was going to come out, but I was willing to go along with her for a while. That's very different from someone who is hostile and withdrawing.

Jeri: She was playful and creative.

Eddi: I felt like the children were playing like four- and seven-year-olds They seemed so much younger than they are.

Ivan: I think these children function at multiple levels. They play like four- and seven-year-olds, and they can also play at fourteen and eighteen, and then they parent their parents.

Mary: It may depend on how old Mother and Father are being.

Ivan: Right. And what is worrying them, and how they personify this to take care of their parents.

Jeri: Mother wore knee-high stockings and the band was showing. Barbara came over and pulled Mother's skirt down so the band didn't show.

Ivan: When Father came back from the bathroom, Barbara said, "your tie is not straight."

Jeri: She straightened his tie.

Ivan: The children relate to one another and their parents on multiple levels. If you observed this family at only one moment in time or in cross-section, you would not get an impression-in-depth of these children. They are remarkable. The little boy played out nonverbally what was going on with other family members at the verbal level. He heard it all and acknowledged his understanding when I said, "I am hearing it all" when I pretended to be him. Then he did something interesting. He hit his head on a chair rhythmically in response to the tension between Mother and daughter. It is important not to be too interested in the so-called pathology like the daughter's stealing because it makes you focus on all the negative content about the family and you miss the richness of the family interactions and their process of relating to each other. By focusing on the interactions themselves and the many levels of communication, as shown by this family, you can better understand the meanings the family gives to each other's actions and words and, hence, their tautological explanations of themselves.

Barry: You made a quite clear decision in the beginning to not spend time on the relationship between the family and therapist. What made you decide to do that?

Jeri: Partly from the simulation. By doing that in the simulation we could see that my first question about why the family was here got Silvia into trouble. She unknowingly told us a family secret. The second clue we got was when I started to ask the daughter what brought them to Silvia. Mother was getting on the brink of telling us what a bad girl Barbara was.

Ivan: This was further confirmed later when Mother said, "Silvia and I are working on . . .," as if it were a private conversation. I tried to open it up with "who else was there?" There were several moments when it was clear that to probe, that is, to deal with that relationship, would have lost Barbara. Yet, not to probe might lose Mother, because she needed to talk about her frustrations. So we had to find another way to bring Mother in. But that had to be very delicate. We had to be careful about how we brought in Silvia. I was very happy about that. I thought Barbara gave a real clear message that there was a privacy that had to be respected.

Jeri: It's a loyalty issue. I didn't know that at the time. It just occurred to me. It was a loyalty issue between Mother and Silvia. Had we found out that Mother cared too much for Silvia, she could have been too vulnerable.

Ivan: (to Silvia) You could also have been the mother-in-law. We needed to keep everything fluid so the therapist did not get stereotyped in this interview as the Mother or as the mother-in-law or as a mother who is really a child or a child who is really a mother. She (Silvia) is the female in this scenario. She is the vulnerable female because she works at many levels of relationships We, as consultants, frame a therapist but must be careful not to box her in inadvertently. Consultants have to be aware of not becoming a part of the problem or creating a problem for the therapist.

Barry: In retrospect, now, could there be a way of addressing the therapist-family relationship as if it was a consultation that wouldn't have gotten you into that position? At the moment you are describing it as an either/or. Could there be a way you could have addressed the nature of that relationship without falling into the difficulties you just described?

Ivan: Do you have something in mind?

Barry: No.

Ivan: In principle yes. But right now I can't imagine it. It could have been done differently. We have done it differently, turned to the therapist and talked to the therapist in a reflective process.

Jeri: Yes, we did it very differently with the last family Silvia brought in for consultation. There was much more openness about her work with them. There weren't as many pitfalls as there were with this family. It may also be the delicacy of the relationship Silvia has with this family. They have only met three times.

Silvia: That is a big part of it. I'm only getting to know the family.

Jeri: It was also a bit of a rush for Silvia to bring this family. There is a fragile bond between the family and Silvia. We were being respectful of that.

Ivan: Sometimes, after a consultation, the therapy explodes because consulting can be such an intrusion and it can put the therapist in an awkward position, whether the therapist supported the view of the consultants or not. It can push the therapy too hard. Another important question for the consultants is how to keep the interview from producing a schismogenesis or runaway situation.

Barry: Tom Andersen talks about introducing too much of a difference or too little of a difference and getting into trouble.

Ivan: Yes, we have to consider the ongoing relationship of consultant to therapist and therapist to family.

Eddi: I thought about the delicate way you were able to relegate the content of the secrets to Silvia. It was like . . . OK we're not going to talk about the content so we will talk about process.

Silvia: They caught on well and it reduced their anxiety.

Ros: I was impressed with the elegance of your work today. I learned from watching you today, something about what you talk about as metaphor. The way you actually create experiences. A co-evolving reality actually is about creating metaphor or action in the session which is very different than I would do. Watching that was very nice and different. I'm very preoccupied with the differences in our work and yours. It raises questions. I just wrote down that I want to go on talking about the way we behave as therapists when we do therapy. How different behaviours as therapists reflect different beliefs But I don't believe we believe different things about intentionality. That was fascinating.

David: I'm going to need to think about this, so I can come up with something a little more thought through. But my initial impression is that I was extremely interested and learned most about the power of restraint in your technique. I found myself saying, at times, Ah! go for that! At other times, ah! go for that! And you didn't. And things happened. I was very impressed by that. I would like to see the tape and look for that technique you used. I learned a lot from that.

Jeri: When you used the word restraint, I thought that is what you do. You use a tremendous amount of restraint but in a very different way.

David: Yes.

Ivan: Yes.

Jeri: That's fascinating because I would have used the very same word to describe your work, and I never see myself as being restrained.

Ivan: We do try to build a common co-evolving metaphor but in incomplete gestalts. So that the mosaic that comes out of the whole process . . .

Jeri: . . . and belongs to the family . . .

Ivan: . . . is their gestalt They make it. The restraint is to help retain the incompleteness of the gestalt so that the family fills in their own blanks. That is what makes metaphor. Two somethings that link and create another class of information, meaning, belief. All of those things together allow them to complete the gestalt.

Doug V.: What stands out most strongly for me has to do with the way you work together. The way you seem to take an idea and transform it. It has meaning for the family at a subliminal level and when you offer it to them, almost as a mirror, they take it and go with it. They go with it animatedly. So either way they take on the idea you offer them. For me that was the most fascinating thing I saw. You took one idea and moved it to another idea and transformed it. The family sat and listened and processed it and, it seemed to me, you addressed the level that was true for them. They recognized it and made the shift with you. The gestalt is what I think it is. That was fascinating for me to see.

Ivan: What Doug is saying is meaningful to me. We work at the level of the family's understandings. We try to find a "fit" with them. If they are into concrete action, we work at the level of concrete action, in action. If they work at the level of abstraction, we work with them in abstraction. That's what happened today. The key idea is to work toward "fit" and to avoid trying to have the family "match" our preconceived standards or ideas. Reciprocally, we also try to avoid submitting to the family's efforts for us to "match" their preconceived standards also. This enhances movement towards co-evolving metaphors and meanings.

Doug V: What seemed to me to happen today, both in the simulation and the interview, is that you pitched at the level that was correct for both systems. That was exciting.

Ivan: We learned from Ros and David how to interview tightly. It looks different. They stay at the same level with the family.

They repeat what somebody said, then they move it. Then they repeat and move it. It's interesting how we have transformed that into our own way and found a language for it.

Doug V: Inclusive you call it.

Jeri: That's the part of letting them fill in the other end of the gestalt.

Ivan: Now we have similarities of difference and differences of similarities.

Paddy: A lot of these ideas seemed strange. What makes them strange is that I don't have any little boxes in my mind to parcel them into. If I tried to understand too rapidly, I would have to create boxes artificially. I would have to just grab a few boxes I have around and pop them into them. It would be a grave injustice. So I ask you to let me have time for new boxes to grow in my mind Grabbing boxes would take away from the value of what I saw.

Jeri: OK.

Ivan: Elegantly put.

Chris F: Could I say how much I admired your ability to tolerate that ambiguity. For example, and there were lots of them, how long was that pause going to last? How long were those children going to be out there before somebody went after them? How long were you going to let that happen? Somehow or other by being able to deal with that ambiguity, you allowed the family to hand that over to you. Only by holding that tension yourselves, in the Kleinian sense, could they then work.

Jeri: Unfortunately, we have to stop our debriefing now. We probably could continue for some time. This family has provided us with much to talk about concerning interviewing methods, beliefs, and the various functions of the interviewers in the context of consultation and therapy.

The update

We trust that this experience has been as interesting for you, the reader, as it has been for us to write about this experience. We want to offer an update about the family so that you can go back and look again, as we have, and see the innuendos and how the parents have played them out in the six months since the interview.

Family therapy can be a very humbling experience when we realize the tremendous force that the process of redundancies of pattern play in all our lives. The pull of the legacies in families and the push of cultural backgrounds makes volitional changes a difficult matter. When a woman has experienced her mother's abandonment by her father, whether by death or divorce, there seems to be a great thrust in her life, which often produces the same circumstances, in spite of the consequences, many of which are known to her. We know that this Mother lost her father when she was seven years old, and she was the youngest child in her family. She experienced her mother as a single-parent and was aware that her grandmother brought her children up alone as well.

In this family, Barbara experienced psychological abandonment at the age of six when Steven was born. Steven is now seven years old, the youngest child in the family, and the fear of divorce is evident about Barbara. The main themes in this interview were secrets and losses.

The update is that both parents were involved in affairs at the time of the interview. Both were in individual psychotherapy at the time as well. Now they are getting a stormy divorce, Mother's mother is moving to Portland to give her the support that she only can give one person, or that she can only give Mother when she is alone.

Silvia attempted to see them as a family, but all these circumstances led her to believe that she could best help the family by supporting Barbara through the divorce. Perhaps she will be supporting Barbara in a way that is similar to the way that Mother's mother will support her. This would put Silvia in the role of surrogate grandmother, a role she has felt pressured to play since the beginning of her relationship with the family.

Barbara's acting out has lessened, and she looks forward to her maternal grandmother's move to Portland. We wonder whether grandmother will be able to support both Mother and Barbara, and we hope that Steven will not be overlooked, as Father seems to have been.

Further
theoretical considerations

Introduction

An important theme of the 1989 Exchange Training Program was the relationship between the content and the process in an interview. The focus was on how therapists utilize that relationship in their work with families. As we have thought about the discussions that took place during the Exchange Program, we have formulated several ideas related to content and process as a recursive (circular) phenomenon. A therapeutic experience incorporates belief systems which constitute the contents of both the family and therapists. The ways in which they go about altering their beliefs is the process of their interactions. The family and therapists attend to what they believe to be the others' intentions, and both formulate interpretations of what they think the others' intentions are in the conversation.

In any dialogic encounter the participants are subject to understanding and reacting to each other's perceived intentions. The intentions and behaviours (verbal and nonverbal) are interpreted, and, on this basis, the dialogue proceeds. As it progresses, participants either revise their interpretations about each other's intentions and behaviours or become "stuck" in their views. To the extent that participants are able to let their views co-evolve, the meanings among them change. To the extent that they are unable to alter their views, then fixed and redundant meanings prevail.

By observing the process that families go through as they interact around content, therapists are able to observe the areas of redundancy or stuckness. By interviewing the family and focusing on process, therapists are able to intervene with novel information about the process and amplify the family's meanings to such a degree that participants are launched into new and different interpretations. By altering the process/content redundancy, therapists can help families change their understandings of each other's intentions and interpretations. When therapists attend to their own process and content, intentions and interpretations, they can be more effective with families because they do not run the risk of supporting any redundancies.

By reflecting upon our own beliefs, interpretations and intentions while interacting with the family around their beliefs, interpretations and intentions, we are able to co-construct new meanings in new and different ways. Examining these intentions and interpretations enhances our understanding of the content/process recursion.

Much of the interaction in this interview concerns the sorting of meanings and the co-construction of new meanings. These ideas form the theoretical foundations of our work (Inger and Inger, 1990b) and are the basis for this last section of the book.

Content/Process, Recursion

Meanings in a therapeutic interaction are constructed from the interplay between the content and the process of the exchange between therapists and family. This construction of the "what" (content) and the "how" (process) is a metaphor which is meaningful to the family and therapists (Inger and Inger, 1990b). These meanings form the context of the interaction. Another way to think of the process/content relationship is to think of process as "holding together" and content as "going forward." They form a recursive (circular) relationship of hold together/go forward, hold together/go forward, hold together/go forward. Out of the double or multiple descriptions formed by the content/process recursion, meanings or metaphoric couplings are constructed according to their fit, and a context develops.

Bateson devoted considerable attention to studying the relationship between classifications of content and descriptions of process (Bateson, 1979, p. 193: Keeney, 1983, p. 40). According to Bateson, meaning evolves out of the circular relationship between content and process, and meanings are results of metaphoric constructions rather than logical or categorical sequences.

> Yes, metaphor. That's how this whole fabric
> of mental interconnections holds together.
> Metaphor is right at the bottom of being alive.
>   [Capra, 1989, p. 77]

Keeney (1989, p. 40), commenting on Bateson's ideas of the content/process recursion, calls the content/process relationship a "dialectic of form and process." It is this dialectic of form and process that constitutes a significant portion of the exchange we call family therapy.

Intentions

On the question of therapists' intentions, Tomm (1987b) indicates that therapists have two general intentions: to understand the system and to facilitate change. In order to further therapists' intentions "to facilitate the family's own self-healing," Tomm uses particular forms of questioning that he calls reflexive. Depending on which of these two intentions therapists embrace at a given time, they will ask different kinds of questions. Tomm (1987a, p. 4) describes the interview as a "series of continuous interventions." He emphasizes the importance of therapists' reflections on their actions, and their awareness of their intentions. Tomm conceptualizes intentionality as "strategizing," a fourth guideline for interviewing (added to the three: hypothesizing, circularity and neutrality offered by the Milan Associates [1980]). He defines strategizing as:

. . . the therapists (or teams) cognitive activity
in evaluating the effects of past actions,
constructing new plans of action, anticipating
the possible consequences of various alternatives,
and deciding how to proceed. . . .
[author's italics: 1987a, p. 6]

Tomm highlights the idea that different types of questions reflect different intentions of the therapists and determine the distinctions they make when interviewing the family. He offers a framework for looking at the intentions of the therapists and the consequences of acting on these intentions. He subscribes to the belief that therapists can only indirectly influence the beliefs of the family. Questions are perturbations and influence pre-existing circular processes.

Tomm (1987a, 1987b, 1988) offers a perspective on how to be a systemic therapist, while at the same time using the function of strategizing. He suggests that systemic therapists are sometimes strategists. Systemic therapists, according to Tomm, are strategic when intending to ask leading and/or confrontational questions, when intending to influence the family in a specific manner and when attempting to be corrective. From Tomm's perspective, one can conclude that therapists can consider themselves strategic and systemic depending on their intentions, on their awareness of those intentions, and on how they utilize their intentions in the therapeutic conversation. This is a both/and point of view about the role of therapists.

At the Family Studies Institute, we see strategizing as the process by which we co-create a "safe-enough" environment with all family members so that a self-healing tautology can develop through dialogue between therapists and family (Inger and Inger, 1990b). We make no commitments to particular therapeutic goals. In those cases where goals become a necessity, we consider ourselves to be in a management or counseling position relative to the family, but not in a therapeutic posture which requires neutrality, or multipartiality. Management and counseling functions both carry with them responsibilities to achieve specific goals. The therapeutic posture, on the other hand, requires that the therapists be in the position of working toward understanding and co-creating a metaphor or tautology with the family. We believe understanding leads to a more intimate contact with others.

It has been our experience that by talking with each other during an interview, we are able to hypothesize about both our intentions and interpretations, by asking each other questions in a way that stimulates the family to listen, reflect, and subsequently comment. This puts us in a process of observing ourselves, observing the family, and being observed throughout the interview. We are aware that this experiencing, observing, and reflecting method can be effective because there are two of us interacting with the family. This sort of reflecting also allows for the flow of the interview to continue as opposed to the disruption of the more formal interventions or reflections of the Andersen team (1987).

Andersen and his associates (1987) attempt to give up the idea of intentional interventions as a way of directing change. Andersen states:

> We have also deliberately avoided interventions
> because family members can so easily believe
> that our intervention is better than what they
> themselves have pictured and explained.
>   [1987, p. 427]

The Andersen team transforms intentionality into the reflecting team's thoughts and musings about the family in order to promote change, rather than direct interventions.

> What we try to emphasize is that every person
> in a stuck system tends to think too much in
> terms of either/or and to compete for the right
> to denote what is the right understanding and
> the right action. The reflecting team tries
> to imply the notion of both/and and neither/nor by
> having members of the reflecting team take this
> stance, and by members of the team underlining
> that what they say is based only on the version of
> the problem that each perceives.
>   [Andersen, 1987, p. 427]

We see here strategizing of a different sort. Complementary words of the reflecting team are juxtaposed on the family's beliefs about itself. Embedded in this complementarity is the therapist's intention to change the attitudes of family members about their epistemology (what they think they know and how they know it) and about the problem they present. Although the ambience of the reflecting team is different from that of other intending styles, in that they are respectful of the family's meaning system, and have a less directive and less value-laden intentionality, it seems to us that the reflecting team's actions contain an intervening intentionality none-theless.

Interpretations

On the question of interpretation, Hirsch (1976, p. 19) points out that the concept of interpretation includes three components: explanation, determining significance, and understanding. The explanation component of interpretation concerns clarifying meaning by defining, describing and giving exposition to an interpretation through narration. Determining the significance of the meaning of an interpretation consists of attempts to place hierarchical and comparative importance or value to ideas, events, and objects. Understanding as a component of interpretation encompasses mental acts of comprehending, discerning, sympathizing, empathizing and other forms of wanting to know the other in relation to oneself. All three components overlap every time we make interpretations.

Traditional psychotherapies, especially psychoanalysis, rely heavily on acts of interpretation on the part of the therapist or analyst and their equivalent acts of insight on the part of the client or analysand. Psychoanalytic interpretations and insights focus on three aspects of the analysis: interpreting resistance, interpreting transference and interpreting content (Menninger and Holzman, 1973, pp. 124–157). All of these acts of interpretation are intended to bring the analysand's internal, subjective reality into line with the external, objective reality of the analyst. There is a presumption of objectivity in these acts of interpretation. Although understanding is always an element in any act of interpretation, mutual acts of understanding and inclusion between analyst and analysand as a significant element of interpretation and healing is not considered a primary aspect of the analysis. The interventions of the analyst through acts of interpretation and the insights of the analysand are considered the primary source of change and healing. These acts of interpretation and the analysand's acceptance of the external, objective reality over the internal, subjective reality are the basis of psychoanalysis.

On the other end of the continuum of interpretation, we emphasize understanding and inclusion over acts of explanation and determining significance. Unlike psychoanalysis and other traditional psychotherapies, we do not subscribe to the belief in the predominant importance of acceptance of an immutable, external reality as a viable vehicle to healing or change. In fact, we do not accept the notion of objectivity. We propose that through dialogue intended to promote understanding and inclusion, new beliefs will be co-created with families, change will take place and conflict over competing realities will not be a primary therapeutic concern or activity.

It is common to settle on explanations, and our determinations of meaning, and treat them as stable or fixed while we neglect understanding. Families come to therapy with fixed explanations and meanings and without understanding the importance of alternative explanations and meanings about their relationships and their behaviour patterns with each other. Therapists come to interviews with hypotheses and interpretations about the family and theoretical frameworks for making these interpretations. We introduce our confusion and uncertainty into the conversation as a way to move away from the family's fixed or stable interpretations about themselves and away from our own preconceived notions or interpretations about the family. In this way we move the conversation toward deeper understandings of explanations and interpretations. By claiming our own confusion , "I'm confused," we nudge the family into a posture of thoughtfulness and more openness about their own explanations and, thus, more clarity emerges as they attempt to clarify themselves to themselves and to us. In order to focus on understanding, we must restrain ourselves from using interpretation as explanation or the determining of significance.

Focusing on understanding promotes the intention to know the others' beliefs and to know others in relation to one's own beliefs, a process of working toward inclusion (Buber, 1965, p. 97; Inger and Inger, 1990b). As family therapists, then, we draw on the concept of inclusion in two ways: first by the way we "open" ourselves to and respond to the family members, and second, by the way we encourage family members to use their own capacity for inclusion with other family members (Shabatay, 1990).*

While restraining ourselves from using explanations and interpretations in traditional therapeutic ways, we nonetheless recognize the importance of the functions of interpretation in creating and holding meanings. Using a co-therapy team in the room with the family allows for interpretations to be used as reflective musings. As a two-person team, we periodically talk to one another in the presence of the family and reflect on our experience with the family. We ask each other questions in the form of a mini-interview, and we discuss our ideas. This dialogue is meant to stimulate thinking on the part of family members. This form of interpretive, reflective musings allows for an ongoing flow between process and content in the interview, without stopping the interaction.

As we have reflected upon our own work, it has become clear to us that we are using strategies. We are strategizing when we restrain ourselves from taking an explanatory position, and we strategize for understanding and inclusion (Inger and Inger, 1990b). We allow the family to provide explanations about which we ask questions, propose new ideas and amplify the old. In this way our understanding becomes a primary function for us while the family struggles with its own explanations and significations and new and different meanings. Understanding for the family can be a by-product of an interaction. Strategizing for understanding may take the form of amplifying polarities for the sake of initial confusion (p. 61) and later expansion of meanings (p. 67), and amplifying the family's metaphors in incomplete gestalts (p. 69). The family can complete the gestalts in new and different ways and, thereby, experience new meanings and their applicability within and outside

---

*Inclusion, a term Martin Buber uses in connection with dialogue, means that one is able to understand what another is feeling in a particular situation and at the same time to grasp one's own feeling about the situation. Inclusion comes to us because we have opened ourselves to the "other" and have come to know him or her. We have "made present" his or her particular being to ourselves. Inclusion is a partaking of relationship, of that world of the "between" where two (or more) people share experiences. It means, as well, that we do not set aside our own views for the sake of others; rather, an open exchange takes place (Shabatay, 1990).

the family. As the reader/observer saw in the presentation, these methods are carried out by the two of us as we work together to construct meaningful conversation with the family members.

By taking the position of ones who seek to understand, we provide a more safe environment for the family while we communicate our respect for the family's struggle with its dilemma(s). The responsibility to bring about change, to explain why the dilemma exists, and how to alleviate it is given to the family. The knowledge that they will maintain responsibility and control in their family becomes a part of the safety that we as therapists can provide. Our responsibility is to try to achieve understanding, provide a safe-enough environment, to respect all members of the family, and to adhere to the belief in the self-healing nature of the family.

Applying Content/Process Recursions and Understanding

As co-consultants in this interview, we value caution. We gradually engage each family member in an exchange so that a "runaway" (schismogenic — see Bateson, 1972, pp. 126–127) situation does not occur. To that end, we try to thread our way delicately through the unknown, but hypothesized, intentions of each family member. Our overriding intention is to ask questions in a way that will include all family members in the dialogue. We want to guard against any members being made to feel like the Identified Patient in the family, which can happen easily when one member is allowed to spew out a litany of negative attributions about another or when questions are asked in a confronting manner. We work hard to keep family members from withdrawing irretrievably from the family therapy.

Our initial intention is to push toward the process end of the recursion and away from content, especially symptomatic content which could be harmful. In this regard we agree with Tomm that:

> To ask about a problem is to invite its
> emergence and to affirm its existence.
> In addition, to listen to and to accept
> the description of a problem is to concede
> power with respect to its definition.
>   [1987a, p. 4]

We use our "selves" to do this. We accept our state of confusion and anxiety; we feel free not to accept the gestalt of the meanings the family offers; we talk with each other to keep our hypotheses fluid and to keep contact with each other; we use "different voices;" and we attempt to keep our sense of humour and lightness in the face of the seriousness brought by the family and still remain respectful of them.

In light of our hypotheses about the intentions of family members to divulge a secret, we chose to interview from a strategy of restraint. Using restraint in this way is a form of strategizing through actions. It is manifested as omissions on the part of the interviewers. Restraint, as we utilize it, is a series of moves into content, stopping short and moving away from content, omitting any conclusions or even further curiosities. It is a recursive rhythm of move in/move out, move in/move out, etc. Restraining in this interview is a blending of curiosity with withdrawing of curiosity at particular moments in the dialogue about specific content. This rhythm encourages a process (go forward) of interaction which is in complement with the content (hold together) being explored. By using restraint, therapists maximize curiosity or multipartiality without risk of being cornered into content-dominated conversation with the family. In an interview we can have many issues of content up in the air at a given time, and none pursued with finality. These actions are part of the content/process recursion we utilize (hold together/go forward) to help co-create a context of conversation. We explore an issue, leave it, move to another, leave it, move to another, leave it, then move back to a previous issue, etc. After a time, we have many threads ready to be woven into a fabric of meaning with the family. Restraint helps avoid any one thread (like a symptom or problem) from becoming too dominant, and changes the importance and meaning of these symptoms which already dominate the life of the family.

Restraint on the part of the therapists is also a way of keeping the fluidity in the conversation, and of keeping the therapists from settling on or being perceived to settle on the significance of meanings by the family or by themselves. The significance of meanings are up to the family and not the therapists. Therapists can reflect on these possible meanings but must be careful not to push for conclusive significance as if it were a final state or "fact."

One of our intentions in an interview is to refrain from closing off constructions of new or revised meanings of old interactions. If therapists become settled on meanings, then they have the tendency to want the family to settle on these interpretations or meanings. This we would consider the therapists' dilemma of trying to have their tautological meanings become the tautological meanings of the family, instead of co-constructed tautologies which are a function of their interactions together (Inger and Inger, 1990b). We subscribe to the belief that the job of therapists is to create a climate for new possibilities for their old meanings and encourage the family towards reconstructions of their patterns of interaction and, hence, reconstructions of new, different or transformed tautologies which are more effective for them.

Conclusion

Moving this interview recursively between content and process gave the family the opportunity to explore relationships across generations. By staying with the content, as they would have had us do, we would have focused on Barbara's dilemma in a way that could have created a push for resolution. Content appeals to all of us as if it was a stationary or fixed reality. It seems comforting to all of us to use content as a means of holding together a particular belief in a "reality." It is more difficult to go forward and to experience change in the content of an experience which seemed to have offered us stability. Process is going forward through experiences and can be the vehicle that changes the meaning of the content of that experience. When we believe in multiple realities and multiple partialities, we have to interview families emphasizing the balance between the content and the process of interactions in order to make it "safe enough" for the multiple realities to emerge. When family members are able to share their ideas as points of view, instead of "truths," they are often able to evoke understanding and compassion for one another.

In order to co-create a new context, we had to interview this family on the edge of the tension between content and process. We had to maintain the tension between our intentions and theirs. We believed that time was an element in the creation of that tension, and we found that, by reflecting aloud to one another, we were able to slow down the dialogue and, thus, create enough *spaces* for the tension to develop. During that time the dialogue was able to move out of content and into process for successively longer periods of time. Like the child in the rapprochement phase of development, the family moved cautiously away from the familiar content, until the self-conscious awareness of the unfamiliar caught up with them. Then, like the child, they returned for a refill of the familiar "stuff." As the anxiety of ending came upon them, they brought the dialogue back to their familiar content by teasing us about their secrets.

Allman, L. R. (1982). The aesthetic preference: Overcoming the pragmatic error. *Family Process*, 21: 43–56.

Andersen, T. (1987). The reflecting team: Dialogue and meta-dialogue in clinical work. *Family Process*, 26: 415–428.

Bateson, G. (1972). *Steps to an Ecology of Mind*. New York: Ballantine.

_____ (1979). *Mind and Nature: A Necessary Unity*. New York: E. P. Dutton.

Buber, M. (1965). *Between Man and Man* (tr. by Ronald G. Smith). New York: Macmillan.

Capra, F. (1989). *Uncommon Wisdom*. New York: Bantam Books.

Hoffman, L. (1985). Beyond power and control: Toward a "second order" family systems therapy. *Family Systems Medicine*, 3: 381–396.

_____ (1990). Constructing realities: An art of lenses. *Family Process*, 29: 1–12.

Hirsch, E. D. (1976). *The Aims of Interpretation*. Chicago: The University of Chicago Press.

Inger, I., and Inger, J. (1990a). The evolution of a multiperson therapeutic system. *Journal of Strategic and Systemic Therapies* (in press).

Inger, I. B. , Inger, J., and Baker, S. (1990b). Family therapy exchange: A cross-cultural affair. *Journal of Strategic and Systemic Therapies* (in press).

Keeney, B. (1983). *Aesthetics of Change.* New York: Guilford Press.

Maturana, H. (1978). Biology of language: The epistemology of reality. In G. A. Miller and E. Lennenberg (Eds.), *Psychology and Biology of Language and Thought: Essays in Honor of Eric Lennenberg.* New York: Academic Press.

Maturana, H., and Varela, F. (1980). *Autopoiesis and Cognition: The Realization of the Living.* Boston: D. Reidel.

Menninger, K. A., and Holzman, P. S. (1973). *Theory of Psychoanalytic Technique* (second edition). New York: Basic Books.

Selvini Palazzoli, M. , Boscolo, L., Cecchin, G., and Prata, G. (1978). *Paradox and Counterparadox.* New York: Jason Aranson.

Shabatay, V. (1990). Personal communication.

Tomm, K. (1985) Circular interviewing: a multifaceted clinical tool. In D. Campbell and R. Draper, *Applications of Systemic Family Therapy: The Milan Approach* (ch. 4, pp. 33-45). London: Grune & Stratton.

_____ (1987a). Interventive interviewing: Part I. Strategizing as a fourth guideline for the therapist. *Family Process,* 26: 3-13,.

_____ (1987b). Interventive interviewing: Part II. Reflexive questioning as a means to enable self-healing. *Family Process,* 26: 167–183.

_____ (1988). Interventive interviewing: Part III. Intending to ask linear, circular, strategic, or reflexive questions? *Family Process,* 27: 1-15.

Varela, F. (1979). *Principles of Biological Autonomy.* New York: North-Holland Press.

von Foerster, H. (1981). *Observing Systems.* Seaside, CA: Intersystems Publications.

von Glasersfeld, E. (1984). An introduction to radical constructivism. In P. Watzlawick (Ed.), *The Invented Reality: How Do We Know What We Believe We Know?* New York: W. W. Norton.